S Corporation Tax Secrets

Maximizing Benefits for Small Business Owners

Ethan Reynolds

Disclaimer

This publication aims to offer knowledgeable and trustworthy information on the subject matter covered. It is offered with the understanding that the author is not giving tax or any other professional advice. A professional should be consulted if taxation or other expert assistance is needed because laws and practices frequently differ from state to state and country to country. The author expressly disclaims any liability resulting from using or applying this book's contents.

TABLE OF CONTENT

strategies

8.3 Taking advantage of S corporation-specific tax breaks and incentives

8.4 Exploring tax deferral strategies

8.5 Putting in place tax-efficient compensation structures

8.6 Harnessing the Power of Employee Perks and Fringe Benefits

8.7 Trusts and Estate Planning: What Role Do They Play?

8.8 Case studies demonstrating sophisticated tax planning strategies

Case Study 1: Income Diversification Strategy

Case Study 2: Tax Credits and Incentives

Case Study 3: Deferred Tax Exchanges

Conclusion

Chapter 9: S Corporation Distributions: Dividends, Loans, and Tax Consequences

Introduction

9.1 Differentiating between dividends and loans in the context of S corporation distributions

9.2 The tax treatment of qualified and non-qualified dividends for S corporation owners

9.3 Calculating the effect of accumulated earnings and personal holding company tax on distributions

9.4 Recognizing the tax implications of shareholder loans and their repayment

9.5 Techniques for structuring tax-advantaged distributions and debt arrangements

9.6 Distribution considerations when liquidating or selling a business

9.7 S corporation distribution compliance with IRS regulations and reporting requirements

9.8 Real-world examples illustrating the tax implications of various distribution scenarios

Scenario 1: Equal Dividend Payments

Scenario 2: Proportional Distributions

Chapter 12: S Corporation Audits and IRS Compliance

Introduction

12.7 Options for appeals and dispute resolution in the event of an unfavorable audit outcome

12.8 Preventive measures to reduce the possibility of future audits and improve compliance

Conclusion

Chapter 13: S Corporation Tax Planning for Changing Circumstances

Introduction

13.1 Recognizing common triggers for changes in S corporation tax planning strategies

13.2 Changing compensation structures and distributions to reflect business growth or decline

13.3 Evaluating the impact of economic factors on tax planning, such as inflation or interest rate changes

13.4 Strategies for navigating changes in tax laws, regulations, and provisions

13.5 Changing retirement planning strategies as business owners approach retirement or face financial changes

13.6 Assessing the tax implications of major business transactions such as mergers, acquisitions, or expansions

13.7 Increasing tax benefits by strategically timing business expenditures and investments

13.8 Reviewing and updating tax planning strategies on a regular basis to ensure ongoing compliance and optimization

Conclusion

Chapter 14: S Corporation State and Local Tax Considerations

Introduction

14.1 Understanding the fundamentals of state and local taxation and its application to S corporations

14.2 Navigating the complexities of state income tax laws and calculating state S corporation tax liabilities

14.3 Considerations for S corporations in multiple states, including nexus and apportionment rules

14.4 Legal and permissible strategies for reducing state and local tax burdens

Chapter 15: International Tax Planning for S Corporation Owners

INTRODUCTION

Welcome to *"S Corporation Tax Secrets: Mastering Benefits for Small Business Owners."* In this comprehensive guide, we will delve into the complexities of S corporation taxation and uncover the valuable strategies and secrets that can help small business owners maximize their tax benefits.

Understanding the tax advantages offered by S corporations is critical to your financial success as a small business owner. S corporations provide a unique structure that allows for pass-through taxation, minimizing the tax burden on business income and maximizing tax savings opportunities. However, navigating the complex landscape of S corporation taxation necessitates knowledge and expertise.

In this book, we will demystify the world of S corporation taxation and provide you with the tools and insights you need to make informed decisions that will benefit both your business and your personal financial goals. Each chapter will delve into a specific aspect of S corporation taxation, from understanding the S corporation structure to maximizing deductions, exploring retirement plan options, and addressing state and local tax considerations.

We will provide practical tips, real-life case studies, and expert advice throughout the book to illustrate the concepts and strategies discussed. Whether you are a seasoned S corporation owner or considering the switch from another entity type, this book will serve as your comprehensive resource to navigate the complex world of S corporation taxation and uncover its hidden benefits.

It is important to note that, while this book provides valuable insights and guidance, consulting with a qualified tax professional is always recommended to ensure compliance with IRS regulations and tailor strategies to your specific circumstances.

So, let's go on this journey together and discover the S corporation tax secrets that will enable you to master the benefits and achieve financial success as a small business owner.

Chapter 1: Understanding the S Corporation Structure

Introduction

S corporations have grown in popularity in the dynamic landscape of small businesses due to their unique tax advantages and flexibility. This chapter provides a thorough understanding of the S corporation structure and its implications for tax planning and savings, making it an essential foundation for small business owners.

Key topics covered in this chapter include:

1. What exactly is an S corporation?
2. The benefits and drawbacks of using an S corporation structure.
3. Eligibility requirements and the formation procedure.
4. Recognize S corporation pass-through taxation.
5. Significant distinctions between S corporations and other types of business entities (such as C corporations and partnerships).
6. Investigating shareholders and their roles in an S corporation.
7. S corporation compliance and reporting requirements.
8. Case studies demonstrating the advantages of using an S corporation structure.

By delving into these fundamental aspects, small business owners will gain a solid foundation of knowledge to guide their decision-making and maximize tax benefits within the realm of S corporations.

1.1 The Definition and Characteristics of an S Corporation

An S corporation is a one-of-a-kind business structure that combines a corporation's limited liability protection with the pass-through taxation of a partnership or sole proprietorship. S corporations, as a result, are not subject to federal income tax at the entity level. Instead, the company's profits and losses are "passed through" to the shareholders, who report them on their personal tax returns.

One of the most important features of an S corporation is the limited liability protection it provides its shareholders. This means that the shareholders' personal assets are generally protected from the business's debts and liabilities. It should be noted, however, that certain exceptions and limitations to limited liability may apply.

1.2 Eligibility Criteria for S Corporation Status

To qualify for S corporation status, a company must meet certain criteria established by the Internal Revenue Service (IRS). These are some of the criteria:

1. **Limited number of shareholders:** Individuals, estates, certain trusts, or tax-exempt organizations may be the only shareholders in a S corporation, and they must be individuals, estates, certain trusts, or tax-exempt organizations. Members of the same family are also treated as single shareholders.

2. **United States residency and citizenship requirements:** S corporations must have shareholders who are citizens or residents of the United States. Non-resident aliens are generally not permitted to own stock in S corporations.

3. **Single class of stock:** S corporations can only have one class of stock, which means that all shares have the same rights to

distributions and liquidation proceeds. Different voting rights are permitted, but economic rights must be consistent.

4. **Limited types of shareholders:** Certain entities, such as partnerships, corporations, and non-resident alien shareholders, are not permitted to be shareholders in S corporations. Certain types of trusts and tax-exempt organizations, on the other hand, may qualify.

1.3 The Benefits of S Corporation Taxation

The pass-through nature of income and losses is one of the primary benefits of S corporation taxation. This means that, unlike C corporations, the profits, and losses of the business are not subject to double taxation. Instead, they are reported and taxed at the individual level on the shareholders' individual tax returns. Small business owners can avoid paying corporate-level taxes on their profits, which can result in significant tax savings.

Another advantage of S corporation taxation is the possibility of tax savings for self-employment. S corporation shareholders who work for the business, unlike sole proprietors and partners in a partnership, are not subject to self-employment taxes on the portion of their income classified as "distributions" rather than salary.

1.4 Employee Shareholders and Compensation

Shareholders who are also employees of an S-corporation must receive reasonable compensation for the services they provide to the corporation. Employment taxes, such as Social Security and Medicare, apply to this compensation. However, any remaining profit distributions to shareholders in excess of their reasonable compensation are exempt from employment taxes.

Determining reasonable compensation can be difficult because it is dependent on a number of factors, including industry norms, the employee's role, and the corporation's financial performance. To ensure compliance with IRS guidelines, it is best to consult with a tax professional.

1.5 Limitations and Considerations of S Corporation Status

While S corporations have many advantages, there are some limitations and considerations to be aware of:

1. **Shareholder restrictions:** The number and type of shareholders that an S corporation can have are limited. This can limit the ability to raise capital and attract new investors.
2. **Income types are restricted:** S corporations are generally restricted in the types of income they can earn. Certain types of passive income, for example, may subject the corporation to an additional tax known as the Passive Income Tax.
3. **Considerations for capital raising:** S corporations may face difficulties in raising capital because they cannot issue different classes of stock or easily attract outside investors.
4. **Compliance requirements:** S corporations are subject to ongoing compliance requirements, such as holding regular shareholder and director meetings, keeping proper corporate records, and filing annual tax returns.

Small business owners can make informed decisions about whether an S corporation is the right choice for their company by understanding the nuances of the S corporation structure, eligibility criteria, and benefits and considerations involved.

1.6 Steps to Form an S Corporation

There are several steps involved in forming an S corporation. While the specific requirements may differ depending on the state in which the business is located, the general process usually entails the following:

Step 1: Choose a business name. For your S corporation, choose a unique and appropriate name. Check that the name follows the state's naming guidelines and does not infringe on any existing trademarks.

Step 2: Prepare and file articles of incorporation with the appropriate state agency. This document formalizes your S corporation and includes important information such as the business name, address, purpose, and number of authorized shares of stock.

Step 3: Obtain all required licenses and permits. Determine which licenses and permits are required to run your business.

Step 4: Establish the stock structure. Determine the number of shares to be issued and their par value. You may also need to consider any stock-related restrictions or special provisions, such as voting rights or preferential treatment.

Step 5: Create and adopt bylaws. Create bylaws that outline your S corporation's internal rules and procedures. These bylaws cover important topics like shareholder meetings, director responsibilities, and the company's decision-making process.

Step 6: Hold an organizational meeting. Hold an initial meeting with shareholders and directors to ratify the bylaws, elect officers, and discuss any other important issues concerning the operation of the S corporation.

Step 7: Obtain the necessary licenses and tax identification numbers. Register your S corporation with state agencies such as the Secretary of State's office. In addition, obtain from the IRS an Employer Identification Number (EIN), which is required for tax purposes.

Step 8: Prepare and distribute stock certificates. Prepare and distribute stock certificates to the initial shareholders, which document their ownership interests in the S corporation.

Step 9: Comply with ongoing obligations. Understand and meet the S corporation's ongoing compliance requirements. This includes keeping proper corporate records, holding regular shareholder and director meetings, and filing annual tax returns with the IRS (Form 1120S).

You can successfully form an S corporation and lay a solid foundation for your small business by following these steps and adhering to the necessary legal and regulatory requirements.

In the following chapters, we will delve deeper into various aspects of S corporation taxation, such as optimizing salary and distributions, maximizing deductions for business expenses and write-offs, enabling S corporation owners to participate in retirement plans, and much more. Understanding these topics will help you navigate the complexities of S corporation taxation and make informed decisions that will benefit your business as well as your personal financial goals.

Chapter 2: Optimizing Salary and Distributions

Introduction

One of the primary advantages of operating as an S corporation is the ability to optimize salaries and distributions, which allows business owners to reduce self-employment taxes while remaining in compliance with IRS regulations. This chapter delves into the complexities of striking the proper balance between reasonable compensation and distributions.

This chapter's main topics include:

1. Becoming acquainted with the concept of reasonable compensation for S corporation owners.

2. Identifying the factors that influence fair compensation.

3. Strategies for determining an appropriate salary in order to reduce self-employment taxes.

4. Examining the effects of salary increases on Social Security and Medicare taxes.

5. Optimizing tax benefits by balancing salary and distributions.

6. The effect of the Tax Cuts and Jobs Act on salaries and distributions.

7. Case studies demonstrating effective strategies for salary and distribution optimization.

8. Best practices for documenting and maintaining records to support salary and distribution decisions.

Small business owners can unlock significant tax savings while remaining in compliance with IRS guidelines by mastering the art of optimizing salaries and distributions.

One of the primary benefits of operating as an S corporation is the flexibility it affords business owners to compensate themselves. This chapter delves into the strategies and considerations for optimizing salary and distributions, allowing S corporation owners to strike a balance between personal income requirements and tax efficiency.

2.1 Understanding Reasonable Compensation

It is critical to have a thorough understanding of reasonable compensation in order to effectively optimize salaries and distributions within an S corporation. The salary that an S corporation owner should receive for the services they provide to the business is referred to as reasonable compensation. It is a critical component of remaining in compliance with IRS regulations and ensuring fairness in income distribution.

Determining reasonable compensation entails evaluating the value of the owner's contributions to the S corporation, taking into account factors such as their skills, experience, responsibilities, and the industry's current market standards for similar positions. It should be noted that reasonable compensation may differ depending on the specific circumstances of each S corporation.

The IRS expects S corporation owners to compensate themselves in the same way they would compensate an unrelated employee in a comparable role. This implies that the salary should be proportionate to the duties performed and the level of expertise required. Paying an unreasonably low salary in order to avoid employment taxes and maximize distributions can raise concerns and potentially lead to an IRS audit.

Market standards are important in determining reasonable compensation. Insights into the appropriate range of compensation for specific roles within the S corporation can be gained by researching industry benchmarks and salary surveys. It is critical to consider factors such as the business's geographic location, size, and the financial performance of the industry as a whole.

S-corporation owners can strike a balance between minimizing employment taxes and ensuring that they are appropriately compensated for their contributions by establishing reasonable compensation. Setting an excessively low salary may result in increased IRS scrutiny and the potential reclassification of distributions as wages, resulting in additional tax liabilities and penalties.

It is best to consult with a tax professional who specializes in S corporation taxation to help you navigate the complexities of determining reasonable compensation. They can offer advice based on industry standards and assist in ensuring compliance with IRS regulations. S corporation owners can optimize their salary and distribution strategies while remaining in compliance with tax laws by understanding and adhering to the concept of reasonable compensation.

2.2 Influential Factors in Determining Fair Compensation

Determining fair compensation within an S corporation entails taking into account a number of influential factors that help establish an appropriate salary that is in line with market standards. These factors provide valuable insights into the owner's role and responsibilities, industry norms, the company's financial performance, and the business's geographic location.

The role and responsibilities of the owner are important factors in determining fair compensation. The owner's level of involvement, expertise, and time commitment in running the business should be carefully evaluated. Owners who actively manage day-to-day operations, make strategic decisions, and contribute their specialized skills should be appropriately compensated. On the other hand, owners with a more passive role or limited involvement may be entitled to a lower salary.

Industry norms serve as a guideline for determining fair compensation. Understanding the typical salary ranges for similar positions in the industry can help ensure that the S corporation's compensation practices are in line with industry standards. Salary surveys, market research, and professional associations can all be useful resources for learning about compensation trends.

Fair compensation is also influenced by the company's financial performance. A company that is expanding and making a lot of money can afford to pay its owners more money. In contrast, a company facing financial difficulties or in the early stages of development may need to be more cautious in setting salaries in order to maintain financial stability.

Another factor to consider is geographical location. Compensation levels can vary greatly between regions and markets. When determining fair compensation, consider the cost of living, local labor market conditions, and regional economic factors. Salary comparisons within the local market aid in ensuring that the S corporation's compensation is competitive and reflects the economic realities of the specific location.

S corporation owners can establish fair compensation that reflects their contributions, aligns with industry norms, considers the financial performance of the business, and accounts for geographic location by evaluating these influential factors. Striking the right compensation balance helps to avoid potential IRS scrutiny, promotes fairness within the company, and ensures that the owners are fairly compensated for their efforts.

A tax professional who specializes in S corporation taxation can provide valuable insights and guidance in navigating these factors. They can assist in analyzing industry benchmarks, reviewing financial data, and taking into account local market conditions in order to determine an appropriate salary that maximizes tax benefits while remaining in compliance with IRS regulations. S corporation owners can make informed decisions about fair compensation for themselves and contribute to the overall success of the business by carefully evaluating the influential factors.

2.3 Strategies for Reducing Self-Employment Taxes

When optimizing salary and distributions within an S corporation, a key goal is reducing self-employment taxes such as Social Security and Medicare. S corporation owners can reduce the portion of their income subject to these taxes by strategically structuring compensation and distributions, potentially resulting in tax savings. Let's look at some effective strategies and considerations for accomplishing this goal.

One strategy is to find a happy medium between salary and distributions. S corporation owners have the option of receiving income as a salary or as profit distributions. Distributions, unlike salaries, are not subject to self-employment taxes. Owners can reduce the portion of their income subject to these taxes by keeping the salary portion reasonable while increasing distributions. However, it is critical to maintain a reasonable salary based on factors such as industry norms and the owner's role and responsibilities, as discussed in Section 2.

Another approach is to consider the timing and frequency of distributions. Owners can manage their tax liability by carefully planning the timing and frequency of distributions. For example, if an owner receives a large distribution during a year with a lower overall income, it may result in a lower self-employment tax burden. Tax savings can be maximized by timing distributions to coincide with lower-income years or through strategic tax planning.

Another way to reduce self-employment taxes is to keep earnings within the corporation. Profits retained within an S corporation are not subject to self-employment taxes until they are distributed as dividends. Owners can defer the tax liability associated with profits by reinvesting them back into the business. To ensure compliance with IRS guidelines on reasonable compensation, it is critical to strike a balance between retaining earnings and maintaining an appropriate level of compensation.

Exploring retirement plan options can also help reduce self-employment taxes. Contributions to certain retirement plans, such as Simplified Employee Pension Individual Retirement Accounts (SEP-IRAs) or 401(k) plans, are tax deductible and can reduce the total taxable income subject to self-employment taxes. S corporation owners who use these retirement plans can not only save for the future but also maximize their tax savings in the present.

It is important to note that, while optimizing salary and distributions can lower self-employment taxes, it must be done within the legal parameters. The salary portion should always be reasonable and commensurate with the owner's services. To withstand potential IRS scrutiny, it is critical to keep proper documentation and records supporting compensation decisions.

When implementing these strategies, it is strongly advised to consult with a qualified tax professional who specializes in S corporation taxation. They can provide personalized advice, analyze your specific financial situation, and assist you in navigating the complex tax rules in order to maximize tax savings while adhering to IRS regulations.

S corporation owners can successfully reduce their self-employment tax burden and optimize their overall tax position by employing effective strategies, carefully evaluating the balance between salary and distributions, considering the timing and frequency of distributions, retaining earnings, and exploring retirement plan options.

2.4 Impact of Salary Increases on Social Security and Medicare Taxes

It is critical to understand the impact of salary increases on Social Security and Medicare taxes when considering salary adjustments within an S corporation. Adjusting the salary can have a direct impact on the tax liabilities of S corporation owners, and being aware of these effects is critical for making informed compensation decisions. Let's look at the implications of salary increases and how they affect S corporation owners' tax obligations.

As the owner of an S corporation, you must pay Social Security and Medicare taxes, also known as FICA taxes. These taxes are calculated using the government-set Federal Insurance Contributions Act (FICA) rates. The Social Security tax rate is applied to a specific income level, whereas the Medicare tax rate is applied to all earned income without regard to income level.

When a person's salary rises, so does the amount subject to Social Security and Medicare taxes. As a result, a more significant portion of your income will be subject to these taxes, potentially resulting in a larger tax liability. It's important to note that both the employer and the employee contribute to these taxes, with the employer bearing the brunt of the burden.

Understanding how salary increases affect Social Security and Medicare taxes can assist S corporation owners in making strategic decisions about their compensation structure. There are a few things to keep in mind:

1. Salary-to-distribution balance: Increasing the salary may result in higher tax liabilities due to the additional FICA taxes. To optimize their tax position, S corporation owners should consider balancing their salary with distributions. Owners can reduce the amount subject to Social Security and Medicare taxes by keeping the salary portion reasonable while increasing distributions.

2. Tax planning and timing: Strategic tax planning can help manage the impact of salary increases on FICA taxes. Owners can align salary adjustments with their overall tax strategy by considering the timing of salary adjustments. Increased salary in a year with lower overall income, for example, may help mitigate the impact of higher FICA taxes.

3. Contributions to retirement plans: An increase in salary may affect the amount that can be contributed to retirement plans such as SEP-IRAs or 401(k) plans. These contributions are tax-deductible and can help reduce the amount of taxable income subject to FICA taxes. S corporation owners should consider the impact of salary increases on their retirement plan contributions and optimize their retirement savings within the context of their overall tax planning.

When considering salary adjustments, it is critical to consult with a qualified tax professional who specializes in S corporation taxation. They can offer tailored advice based on your specific financial situation and assist you in navigating the complexities of tax laws and regulations.

S corporation owners can make informed decisions about their compensation structure by understanding the effects of salary increases on Social Security and Medicare taxes. Balancing salary and distributions, strategic tax planning, and taking retirement plan contributions into account can all help to maximize tax savings while remaining in compliance with applicable tax regulations.

2.5 Balancing Salary and Distributions for Optimal Tax Benefits

The right balance of salary and distributions is critical for maximizing tax benefits in an S corporation. S corporation owners can reduce their tax liabilities while still providing reasonable compensation by carefully managing the allocation of income between salary and distributions. Let's look at the significance of salary and distribution balancing and how it can lead to optimal tax savings and financial flexibility within your S corporation.

1. **Reduce self-employment taxes:** One of the primary goals of salary and distribution balancing is to reduce self-employment taxes, including Social Security and Medicare taxes. S corporation owners can reduce the portion of income subject to these taxes by keeping the salary portion reasonable and distributing profits through distributions. Distributions can provide a tax advantage over salary because they are not subject to self-employment taxes.

2. Considerations for reasonable compensation: While optimizing tax savings is critical, it is also critical to ensure that the salary portion reflects reasonable compensation for the services provided. The amount that an S corporation owner should receive for their work should be reasonable, taking into account factors such as industry standards, roles and responsibilities, and the company's financial performance. It is critical to strike a balance between lowering taxes and following the IRS guidelines for reasonable compensation.

3. Income management flexibility: Balancing salary and distributions provides financial flexibility within an S corporation. Owners can gain more control over their personal cash flow by allocating income through distributions. Distributions can be modified based on the company's profitability, cash reserves, and the financial needs of the individual owner. This adaptability enables S corporation owners to respond to changing business conditions and personal financial goals.

4. Tax planning and individual circumstances: The optimal salary-to-distribution ratio varies according to individual circumstances and tax planning strategies. When determining the appropriate mix of salary and distributions, consider factors such as the owner's overall tax situation, retirement plans, and other income sources. Working closely with a qualified tax professional is essential to ensuring that the allocation chosen aligns with your specific financial goals and is compliant with applicable tax regulations.

5. Documentation and record-keeping: When balancing salary and distributions, proper documentation and record-keeping are critical. It is critical to keep detailed records of the services provided, time spent on business activities, and the basis for determining reasonable compensation in order to demonstrate compliance with IRS guidelines. Furthermore, keeping accurate records of distributions and their purposes aids in the taxation of these payments.

Achieving the optimal salary-to-distribution ratio necessitates careful consideration of a number of factors, including self-employment taxes, reasonable compensation, financial flexibility, and individual circumstances. Working closely with a knowledgeable tax professional who can provide guidance tailored to your specific situation is recommended. Their knowledge can assist you in navigating the complexities of S corporation taxation and ensuring that your salary and distribution decisions align with both tax savings goals and compliance requirements.

2.6 The Tax Cuts and Jobs Act: Impact on Salaries and Distributions

Proper documentation and record-keeping are essential for backing up salary and distribution decisions. We will discuss best practices for documenting compensation decisions, keeping records, and adhering to IRS regulations. You can reduce risks and ensure proper documentation in the event of an audit by implementing these practices.

The Tax Cuts and Jobs Act (TCJA), enacted in 2017, made significant changes to the tax code, including provisions that directly affect S corporation owners' salaries and distributions. Understanding these provisions is critical for adapting your strategies and optimizing your tax planning within the framework of the TCJA. Let's look at how the TCJA affects salaries and distributions for S corporation owners.

1. Lower corporate tax rates: One of the most significant changes brought about by the TCJA is a reduction in corporate tax rates. With lower tax rates for C corporations, S corporation owners may need to reconsider their salary and distribution strategies. Because corporate tax rates have been reduced, it is critical to assess the overall tax implications of various compensation strategies and determine the most tax-efficient approach.

2. Qualified Business Income (QBI) Deduction: As part of the TCJA, the QBI deduction was introduced, which provides a potential tax benefit for pass-through entities such as S corporations. This provision allows eligible taxpayers to deduct up to 20% of their qualified business income. However, depending on the owner's taxable income, the nature of the business, and other factors, certain limitations and thresholds apply. Understanding the QBI deduction's rules and requirements is critical when optimizing salary and distributions to maximize this tax benefit.

3. Individual tax rate changes: The TCJA also changed individual tax rates, affecting the taxation of both salary and distributions for S corporation owners. When determining the optimal mix of salary and distributions, it is critical to consider how the revised tax brackets and rates affect overall tax liabilities. Evaluating the new tax rates can help guide compensation and distribution decisions to achieve the best tax outcomes.

4. State and local tax deduction limits: The TCJA imposed limits on the deduction of state and local taxes (SALT). This change may have an impact on the after-tax income of S corporation owners, potentially influencing salary and distribution decisions. Owners should consider the reduced deductibility of state and local taxes when calculating their overall tax burden and allocating income between salary and distributions.

5. Other factors to consider: The TCJA contains a number of provisions that may have an indirect impact on S corporation owners, such as changes to depreciation rules, limitations on business interest deductions, and changes to certain deductions and credits. These provisions may have an impact on S corporation owners' financial situation and tax planning strategies. A knowledgeable tax professional is required to fully comprehend the complexities of the TCJA and its effects on salaries and distributions.

Understanding the specific TCJA provisions that affect salaries and distributions is critical for optimizing tax planning in the new tax landscape. S corporation owners can make informed decisions and adjust their compensation strategies to minimize tax liabilities while remaining compliant with the revised tax regulations by staying informed about the changes brought about by the TCJA. Working with a qualified tax professional to navigate the complexities of the TCJA and tailor your salary and distribution decisions to your specific circumstances is highly recommended.

2.7 Case Studies: Effective Salary and Distribution Optimization

In this section, we will look at real-world case studies that demonstrate effective salary and distribution optimization strategies. These case studies provide practical insights into decision-making and demonstrate successful approaches that can be applied to various business scenarios. Examining these examples will provide you with useful information and inspiration for implementing strategies to optimize your own salary and distribution decisions. Let's look at a few examples of effective salary and distribution optimization techniques:

Case Study 1: The New Startup

Scenario: A newly formed S corporation in the technology sector is attempting to strike a balance between tax efficiency and cash flow management while attracting and retaining top talent. The owner considers various compensation strategies in order to reduce employment taxes while still providing competitive pay to employees.

Approach: Based on industry standards and employee responsibilities, the owner decides to structure the compensation plan by setting a reasonable salary. To reduce employment taxes, the owner employs a combination of salary and distributions. By maintaining a reasonable salary, the owner reduces the portion subject to Social Security and Medicare taxes while adhering to IRS guidelines. The remainder of the profits are distributed as dividends, which are exempt from employment taxes.

Outcome: This strategy lowers employment taxes for both the owner and the employees while maintaining a competitive compensation structure. In a competitive market, the optimized salary and distribution strategy enables the company to allocate funds efficiently and attract top talent.

Case Study 2: The Established Family Business

Scenario: A long-standing family business structured as an S corporation aims to pass wealth down to future generations while minimizing tax burdens. The owners want to maximize distributions so that family members who are not actively involved in the business can receive income.

Approach: The owners collaborate with their tax advisor to create a comprehensive plan that includes salary optimization and strategic distributions. Based on their roles and responsibilities, they determine reasonable compensation for active family members involved in the business. The owners use a combination of salary, dividends, and other distribution methods to provide income for non-active family members. They carefully consider the tax implications of various distribution strategies, taking into account each family member's individual tax bracket as well as any applicable gift and estate tax considerations. This enables them to transfer wealth effectively while minimizing the overall tax burden.

Outcome: The family business achieves its goals of passing on wealth to future generations while minimizing tax liabilities by implementing an optimized salary and distribution strategy. The strategic allocation of income ensures financial support for non-active family members while maximizing tax savings for the entire family unit.

Case Study 3: High-Growth Company

Scenario: The challenge for a rapidly expanding S corporation in the healthcare industry is to manage tax obligations while reinvesting profits to fuel future growth. The owners want to optimize salary and distributions to balance tax efficiency and the business's financial needs.

Approach: The owners collaborate with their financial advisors to develop a tax-efficient compensation strategy. They examine the company's cash flow needs, future growth plans, and tax implications. They determine an appropriate salary for active owners and key employees based on market standards and the company's financial performance. They strategically allocate distributions to support ongoing growth, taking into account the impact on the company's financial stability and future investment opportunities.

Outcome: The optimized salary and distribution strategy enables the high-growth company to effectively manage its tax obligations while reinvesting profits for future growth. By aligning compensation with industry standards and making strategic distribution decisions, the company strikes a balance between tax efficiency and financial needs, allowing it to grow and succeed over the long term.

2.8 Best Practices for Documenting and Maintaining Records

In this section, we'll look at the best practices for documenting and keeping track of salary and distribution decisions. Proper documentation and record-keeping are critical for supporting compensation decisions and ensuring compliance with IRS requirements. You can reduce risks, demonstrate the reasonableness of your compensation decisions, and have a well-documented trail in the event of an audit by implementing these best practices. Let's look at some of the most important best practices:

1. Establish Written Compensation Policies: Create written compensation policies that outline the criteria and factors taken into account when determining reasonable compensation. Clearly define each position's roles and responsibilities, as well as industry standards, financial performance benchmarks, and any other relevant factors influencing compensation decisions. This documentation will be used to justify your compensation practices.

2. Market Research and Benchmarking: Conduct regular market research to learn about current salary ranges for similar positions in your industry and geographic area. To gather data and benchmark your compensation practices against industry standards, use reputable salary surveys, industry associations, and professional networks. To demonstrate the reasonableness of your compensation decisions, document the sources of your market research.

3. Keep a record of Board Resolutions or Meeting Minutes: Hold regular meetings of the board of directors or shareholders and document the compensation discussions and decisions. Keep track of the factors considered, market research findings, and compensation decisions. These meeting minutes or board resolutions serve as official records of your compensation decisions, demonstrating a deliberate and thoughtful approach.

4. Establish Written Employment Agreements or Contracts: Create written employment agreements or contracts for key employees and shareholder-employees. The terms of employment, including job responsibilities, performance expectations, and compensation arrangements, should be clearly defined in these agreements. Formal amendments should be used to document any changes to compensation agreements or employment terms.

5. Maintain a Comprehensive Record of Documents Supporting Your Compensation Decisions: Keep a comprehensive record of documents supporting your compensation decisions, such as salary surveys, industry research, financial performance reports, and individual performance evaluations. Keep payroll records, tax filings, and any other documents that show the consistency and reasonableness of your compensation practices. Organize and store these records in a safe and easy-to-access location.

6. Seek Professional Advice: Consult with a qualified tax professional or accountant who specializes in S corporation taxation. They can provide valuable guidance on IRS regulations, assist in evaluating the reasonableness of compensation decisions, and aid in the implementation of effective record-keeping practices.

By following these best practices for documenting and maintaining records, you will create a solid foundation for justifying your compensation decisions, ensure compliance with IRS requirements, and reduce the risk of potential challenges or audits. Proper documentation not only demonstrates the reasonableness of your compensation practices but also improves transparency and provides a thorough trail of your decision-making process.

Chapter 3: Maximizing Deductions: Business Expenses and Write-Offs

Introduction

In Chapter 3, we'll look at maximizing deductions for business expenses and write-offs for S corporation owners. You can maximize your deductions and reduce your overall tax liability by understanding the wide range of deductible expenses available to you and implementing effective tax planning strategies. This chapter will provide you with the information and tools you need to make educated decisions and maximize your tax savings.

Key topics covered in this chapter include:

1. Overview of deductible business expenses, including operating expenses, advertising costs, rent, utilities, and more.
2. Identifying commonly overlooked deductions specific to S corporations.
3. Strategies for deducting business start-up costs and organizational expenses.
4. Navigating the rules and limitations for meal and entertainment deductions.
5. Understanding the home office deduction and its requirements for S corporation owners.
6. Depreciation rules and strategies for maximizing deductions on business assets.
7. Special deductions and tax breaks for specific industries.
8. Record-keeping tips and documentation requirements to substantiate deductions.

By familiarizing themselves with the breadth of deductible business expenses and mastering the art of maximizing write-offs, small business owners can significantly reduce their tax liability and enhance their financial position.

3.1 Overview of Deductible Business Expenses

In this section, we will go over all of the different types of business expenses that are typically deductible for S corporation owners. Understanding the scope of deductible expenses will provide you with valuable insights into the types of expenses that can help you reduce your tax liability. Let's look at some of the most common types of deductible expenses:

1. **Operating Expenses:** Operating expenses include a wide range of costs that are directly related to the operation of your business. This can include office rent, utilities, insurance premiums, maintenance and repairs, office supplies, and technology costs. You can offset your taxable income and lower your overall tax burden by deducting these operating expenses.

2. **Advertising and Marketing Expenses:** Advertising and marketing expenses are generally deductible. Print or digital advertisements, website development and maintenance, social media marketing, promotional events, and public relations activities are all included. Deducting these expenses can help you promote your business more effectively while also lowering your tax liability.

3. **Rent and lease expenses** are generally deductible if you lease or rent space for your business operations, such as office

space or a retail location. This deduction can result in significant tax savings, especially if rent constitutes a significant portion of your business expenses.

4. **Utilities and Communication Expenses:** Utilities such as electricity, water, gas, and telephone services that are directly related to your business operations are typically deductible. This includes internet and cell phone costs incurred primarily for business purposes. Deducting these expenses can help you reduce your taxable income and maximize your overall tax savings.

5. **Office Supplies and Equipment:** Purchases of office supplies, furniture, computers, printers, and other equipment required for your business can be deducted as business expenses. Keeping track of and deducting these expenses can help offset your taxable income and reduce your tax liability.

6. **Professional Fees and Services:** Legal, accounting, consulting, and other professionals' fees for services directly related to your business are generally deductible. Legal advice, accounting services, tax preparation fees, and consulting fees are examples of these costs. Deducting these professional fees can help you manage your business more efficiently while also lowering your tax liability.

Understanding the extensive list of deductible business expenses available to S corporation owners enables you to identify potential deductions and maximize your tax savings. You can ensure that you are taking full advantage of all eligible deductions and optimizing your overall tax position by carefully tracking and documenting these expenses.

3.2 Identifying Frequently Ignored Deductions

This section will highlight commonly overlooked S-corporation-specific deductions. These deductions, which business owners frequently overlook, can offer significant opportunities to lower your tax liability. You can maximize your tax benefits and optimize your overall tax position by becoming aware of these deductions. Let's look at some of the frequently overlooked S corporation deductions:

1. **Qualified Business Income (QBI) Deduction:** The Tax Cuts and Jobs Act included a valuable deduction known as the Qualified Business Income (QBI) deduction. It allows S corporation owners who qualify to deduct up to 20% of their qualified business income. This deduction, which can provide significant tax savings, is frequently overlooked or misunderstood. Understanding the QBI deduction's requirements and limitations can help you make the most of this tax break.

2. **Health Insurance Premiums:** S corporation owners who pay for their own health insurance premiums may be able to deduct these premiums as a business expense. This deduction can cover the owner's, spouse's, and dependents' health, dental, and long-term care insurance premiums. To qualify for this deduction, the insurance plan must be properly structured and meet certain criteria.

3. **Contributions to Retirement Plans:** S corporation owners can use various retirement plans, such as SEP-IRAs, SIMPLE IRAs, or 401(k) plans, to save for retirement while also reducing their taxable income. Contributions to these retirement plans are typically tax-deductible, allowing you to reduce your tax liability while also securing your financial future.

4. **Home Office Deduction:** You may be eligible for the home office deduction if you use a portion of your home exclusively for your S corporation business. This deduction allows you to deduct a portion of your home-related expenses, such as rent, utilities, insurance, and maintenance costs, based on the percentage of your home that is used for business. It is critical to properly document your home office and meet the IRS's specific requirements in order to claim this deduction.

5. **Bad Debts:** If your S corporation sells goods or provides services on credit and incurs uncollectible debts, you may be able to deduct these bad debts as a business expense. This deduction allows you to write off uncollectible debts, lowering your taxable income.

6. **Business Travel Expenses:** Business travel expenses, such as transportation, lodging, meals, and other incidentals, can be deducted if they are directly related to your S corporation's business. To claim these deductions, you must keep accurate records and follow IRS guidelines.

You can maximize your tax benefits and minimize your tax liability by identifying and understanding these frequently overlooked deductions. To determine your eligibility for these deductions and to ensure compliance with IRS regulations, it is recommended that you consult with a tax professional.

3.3 Methods for Deducting Startup and Organizational Expenses

Starting a business entails initial expenses known as start-up costs and organizational expenses. Market research, legal fees, advertising, employee training, and incorporation costs are examples of these expenses. Properly deducting these expenses can result in significant tax savings for S corporation owners. In this section, we'll go over the rules and strategies for deducting start-up costs and organizational expenses, so you can maximize your deductions and reduce your tax burden in the early stages of your business.

1. **Deduction for Start-up Costs:** The IRS allows you to deduct up to $5,000 in start-up costs in the year that your business begins operations. This deduction, however, begins to phase out once your total start-up costs exceed $50,000. Any remaining start-up costs that exceed the threshold must be amortized over a 180-month (15-year) period. To ensure proper deduction and amortization, it is critical to correctly identify and categorize your start-up costs.

2. **Deduction for Organizational Expenses:** Organizational expenses are the costs incurred in forming your S corporation, such as legal fees for drafting the articles of incorporation,

state filing fees, and fees paid to professionals for business structure organization. Similarly to start-up costs, you can deduct up to $5,000 in organizational expenses in the year your business begins operations, with the deduction gradually phased out once total expenses exceed $50,000. Any excess organizational expenses must be amortized over a 180-month period.

3. **Amortization of Start-up and Organizational Expenses:** If the initial deduction limit is exceeded, the excess amount must be amortized over 180 months. This means that you can deduct a portion of your remaining expenses every year for the next 15 years. Keep track of the amortization schedule and include the deductible portion of these expenses on your annual tax returns.

4. **Proper Documentation:** It is critical to keep accurate records and supporting documentation in order to substantiate your deductions for start-up costs and organizational expenses. Keep invoices, receipts, contracts, and other documents that show the nature and purpose of the expenses. This documentation will be necessary in the event of an audit and will aid in establishing the legitimacy of the deductions.

5. **Speak with a Tax Professional:** It can be difficult to navigate the rules and regulations governing the deduction of start-up costs and organizational expenses. It is strongly advised that you consult with a tax professional who specializes in small business taxation to ensure that you are taking full advantage of the available deductions and following IRS guidelines.

You can effectively deduct your start-up costs and organizational expenses by using these strategies and adhering to IRS rules, lowering your taxable income and maximizing your tax savings. Remember to keep detailed records and seek personalized advice from a tax professional tailored to your specific business situation.

3.4 Navigating the Meal and Entertainment Deduction Rules and Limitations

Deducting meal and entertainment expenses requires careful consideration of the IRS's rules and limitations. We will walk you through the complexities of deducting these expenses, including the substantiation requirements, percentage limitations, and business purpose criteria, in this section. Understanding these rules will help you ensure that you are correctly deducting eligible expenses while adhering to IRS guidelines.

1. **Requirements for Documentation:** The IRS requires adequate documentation to support meal and entertainment expenses. Keeping records that show the amount spent, the date, the location of the expense, the business purpose, and the individuals involved is part of this. Receipts, invoices, and other supporting documents should be kept to prove the expenses claimed on your tax return.

2. **Percentage Limits:** Meal and entertainment expenses are generally limited to a 50% deduction. This means that you can deduct only half of the total expense as a business expense on your tax return. It is critical to distinguish between the

business portion of the expense and any personal or non-deductible portion.

3. **Criteria for Business Purpose:** To be deducted, meal and entertainment expenses must have a clear business purpose. The expense must be directly related to or associated with the active conduct of your business meetings, discussions, negotiations, or other business-related activities. It is critical to document the business purpose and keep records that show the link between the expense and your business activities.

4. **Entertainment vs. Business Meals:** It's critical to differentiate between entertainment and business meal expenses. Tickets to sporting events or concerts, for example, are generally not deductible unless they fall within certain exceptions, such as immediately preceding or following a substantial business discussion. Business meals, on the other hand, may be deductible if they meet certain criteria, such as being held in a business setting and serving a business purpose.

5. **Exceptions and Special Rules:** Meal and entertainment expenses may be subject to certain exceptions and special rules. Employee meals provided on the employer's premises for the employer's convenience, for example, may qualify for a higher deduction percentage. Meals provided to employees at company events or for the benefit of the employer's business are also tax deductible.

6. **Consult with a Tax Professional:** Due to the complexities of the rules and limitations surrounding meal and entertainment deductions, it is highly recommended that you consult with a tax professional. They can provide guidance tailored to your company's needs and assist you in navigating IRS requirements, ensuring accurate deductibility of eligible expenses while reducing the risk of non-compliance.

You can maximize your deductions while remaining in compliance with the IRS guidelines by understanding and adhering to the rules and limitations for meal and entertainment deductions. To ensure accurate and compliant tax reporting, keep detailed records, separate business and personal expenses, and seek professional advice as needed.

3.5 Understanding the Home Office Deduction and Its Requirements for S Corporation Owners

The home office deduction can be a valuable tax-saving opportunity for S corporation owners who conduct business from their home office. In this section, we will delve into the requirements and calculations involved in claiming the home office deduction, enabling you to maximize your tax benefits while meeting the specific requirements for S corporation owners.

1. **Exclusive and Regular Use Test:**

   To be eligible for the home office deduction, the space in your home must be used exclusively and regularly for your business. The term "exclusive use" refers to the use of a designated area solely for business purposes and not for personal use. The term "regular use" refers to the space being used on a consistent basis for your business activities.

2. Calculation Methods: Simplified vs. Regular Method:

The home office deduction can be calculated in two ways: the simplified method and the regular method.

- Simplified Method: Using the IRS-set predetermined rate, multiply the square footage of your home office to determine the deduction. This method is simpler and requires less record-keeping than the regular method, but it may result in a lower deduction.

- The regular method entails calculating the actual expenses related to your home office, such as mortgage interest, property taxes, utilities, and maintenance costs. These costs are prorated based on the percentage of your home that is used for business. The regular method necessitates more meticulous record-keeping, but it may result in a larger deduction if you have significant home office expenses.

3. Specific Requirements for S Corporation Owners:

There are additional requirements to consider as an S corporation owner when claiming the home office deduction:

- Calculation Method: For S corporation owners, the home office deduction is generally based on the percentage of the home used for business purposes multiplied by the corresponding business expenses, such as mortgage interest and utilities. This calculation takes into account the S corporation's ownership percentage.

- <u>Reasonable Rent:</u> If you rent out your home to your S corporation, you must ensure that the rent is reasonable and reflects fair market value. The S corporation should deduct the rent expense as a legitimate business expense.

4. **Documenting Your Home Office:**

   When claiming the home office deduction, proper documentation is critical. Keep records that prove the space's exclusive and regular use, such as photographs, floor plans, or a written description. Maintain records of all expenses related to your home office, such as bills, receipts, and mortgage statements.

5. **Seek Professional Help:**

   Navigating the home office deduction can be difficult, particularly for S corporation owners. It is best to consult with a tax professional who can walk you through the requirements, calculations, and documentation needed to accurately claim the deduction. They can assist you in complying with IRS guidelines and maximizing your tax benefits.

You can take full advantage of this tax-saving opportunity if you understand the requirements and calculations involved in claiming the home office deduction as an S corporation owner. To ensure accurate and compliant tax reporting, remember to meet the exclusive and regular use test, select the appropriate calculation method, keep proper documentation, and seek professional advice as needed.

3.6 Depreciation Rules and Strategies for Maximizing Business Asset Deductions

Depreciation of business assets, such as equipment, vehicles, and machinery, allows for ongoing deductions that can significantly reduce your tax liability. In this section, we'll look at the depreciation rules and strategies available to S corporation owners, so you can maximize your deductions and save money on taxes.

1. Modified Accelerated Cost Recovery System (MACRS):

For most business assets, the Modified Accelerated Cost Recovery System (MACRS) is the primary depreciation method. It gives each asset a specific recovery period based on its classification, allowing you to deduct a portion of the asset's cost over time. MACRS provides a predetermined depreciation schedule that takes into account the asset's useful life as well as the applicable recovery period.

Bonus depreciation is an additional deduction that allows businesses to accelerate the depreciation of certain assets. You can deduct a larger percentage of the asset's cost in the year it is placed in service under this provision. Bonus depreciation percentages may differ depending on the tax laws in effect, so it's critical to stay up to date on current regulations to fully benefit from this deduction.

2. Section 179 Expensing:

Section 179 expensing allows businesses to deduct the full cost of qualifying assets in the year they are placed in service, up to a certain dollar limit. This deduction is especially advantageous for small and medium-sized businesses because it provides immediate and substantial tax savings. However, there are limits to the total amount of Section 179 expensing that can be claimed each year, so keep this in mind when making asset purchases.

3. Depreciation Strategies:

Consider the following strategies to maximize your deductions on business assets:

- Strategic Timing: Consider when to buy assets to take advantage of favorable depreciation rules and provisions. Depending on the current tax laws, it may be advantageous to put assets into service during specific tax years to maximize deductions.

- Asset Classification: Understand the various asset classes and their respective MACRS recovery periods. Proper asset classification ensures accurate depreciation calculations and allows you to make informed decisions when purchasing new assets.

- Cost Segregation: Consider conducting a cost segregation study, especially for larger and more complex assets. This study identifies property components that can be classified as shorter-lived assets and thus qualify for accelerated depreciation deductions.

- Disposal Planning: Create a strategy for disposing of assets in order to maximize depreciation deductions. Understanding the rules and limitations surrounding asset sales or retirements can assist you in effectively planning your asset acquisition and disposal strategies.

- Documentation and record-keeping: Accurate records are essential for depreciation purposes. Maintain meticulous records of asset purchases, including invoices, receipts, and supporting documentation. Document any improvements or modifications made to assets that may have an impact on their depreciable basis.

- Seek Professional Advice: Because depreciation rules and strategies are so complex, it is best to consult with a tax professional who specializes in depreciation and asset management. They can advise on the most advantageous depreciation methods, assist in identifying potential tax savings opportunities, and ensure IRS compliance.

Understanding the depreciation rules and employing effective strategies, such as MACRS, bonus depreciation, and Section 179 expensing, can help you maximize your business asset deductions and maximize your tax savings. To maximize your depreciation deductions, stay up to date on changes in tax laws, keep accurate records, and seek professional advice.

3.7 Industry-Specific Deductions and Tax Benefits

Certain industries qualify for special deductions and tax breaks based on their unique characteristics or contributions to specific industries. This section will go over these industry-specific deductions, allowing you to take advantage of the tax benefits available to your specific industry.

1. **Deductions for Energy Efficiency:**

Industries involved in energy conservation and renewable energy production may be eligible for energy-efficient deductions. These tax breaks encourage companies to invest in energy-efficient equipment, facilities, and technologies. You can reduce your tax liability while promoting sustainable practices in your industry by taking advantage of these deductions.

2. **Credits for Research and Development (R&D):**
   Many industries conduct research and development in order to innovate, improve products or processes, and remain competitive. Research and Development (R&D) credits offer tax breaks for qualifying R&D expenses. These credits can significantly offset the costs of R&D, thereby stimulating innovation and technological advancements in your industry.

3. **Section 199 Qualified Production Activities Deduction:**
   Certain industries, such as manufacturing, construction, and software development, may be eligible for the Section 199 Qualified Production Activities Deduction. By providing a deduction based on qualified production activities income, this deduction encourages domestic production and job creation. You can maximize your deduction and support the growth of your industry by understanding the specific criteria and calculations involved.

4. **Industry-Specific Tax Credits:**
   Specific tax credits are available to various industries in order to promote growth, investment, or specific public policy goals. These credits may include incentives for hiring specific

individuals, investing in underserved communities, or supporting environmental initiatives. Investigate the available tax credits for your industry to identify potential tax savings.

5. **Compliance and Documentation:**

   It is critical to understand and comply with the IRS's specific requirements when claiming industry-specific deductions and tax breaks. To prove your eligibility for these deductions, keep detailed records of your expenses, activities, and supporting documentation. To ensure proper compliance and maximize your tax benefits, consult with a tax professional who specializes in your industry.

6. **Ongoing Industry Research:**

   Tax laws and regulations change over time, and new deductions or incentives for specific industries may be introduced. Keep up to date on industry-specific tax updates and changes in order to identify new opportunities for deductions or tax breaks. Industry associations, tax advisors, and government resources can all be helpful in keeping you up to date.

You can reduce your tax burden and support the growth of your business by researching and understanding the industry-specific deductions and tax breaks available to your industry. To ensure compliance and maximize your tax savings, conduct research, consult with industry experts, and keep accurate records.

3.8 Record-Keeping Suggestions and Documentation Requirements to Support Deductions

Maintaining accurate records and documentation is critical for substantiating deductions and meeting IRS requirements. We will provide helpful hints and best practices for effective record-keeping, organization, and documentation in this section. By following these guidelines, you will be able to confidently support your deductions and be well-prepared for an audit.

1. **Maintain Extensive Records:**

   Keep meticulous records of all business expenses, including receipts, invoices, canceled checks, and any other relevant documents. The nature, date, and amount of each expense should be clearly indicated in these records. Maintaining a digital or physical file for each expense category can aid in record-keeping and retrieval when needed.

2. **Separate Personal and Business Expenses:**

   Separating personal and business expenses is critical for accurately tracking and substantiating deductions. Separate bank accounts and credit cards should be used for business expenses to help distinguish between personal and business transactions. To avoid confusion and ensure accurate deduction claims, clearly label and categorize expenses.

3. **Capture Necessary Information:**

   Make certain that your documentation contains all relevant information. This includes the vendor's name, transaction date, expense description, and purpose of expenditure.

Annotating receipts or attaching additional notes to each expense can provide additional clarity and context.

4. **Consider Accounting Software or Digital Tools:**
   Accounting software or digital tools can help you streamline your record-keeping process. These tools can help you automatically track and categorize expenses, generate reports, and keep a digital archive of your financial records. This can save time, reduce errors, and make your documentation more accessible.

5. **Keep Documentation for the Appropriate Timeframe:**
   The IRS requires you to keep records that support your tax returns for a certain period of time. In general, you should keep records for at least three years from the date you filed your tax return, but certain circumstances may necessitate longer retention periods. To ensure compliance with record retention requirements, consult IRS guidelines or seek advice from a tax professional.

6. **Organize Documentation by Category:**
   Categorize your expenses to organize your documentation in a systematic manner. This can include categorizing expenses such as advertising, office supplies, travel, and equipment purchases. This organization will make it easier to access specific records when they are needed and will aid in the substantiation of deductions during an audit.

7. **Consult a Tax Professional:** Seek advice from a qualified tax professional who can provide personalized advice and ensure

that you are in compliance with IRS regulations. They can advise you on industry-specific requirements, tax-saving strategies, and record-keeping best practices that are specific to your company and circumstances.

8. **Maintain Compliance with IRS Regulations:**
   Tax laws and regulations change on a regular basis, and IRS guidelines may be revised. Keep up-to-date on the latest record-keeping requirements to ensure that your practices are compliant with current regulations. The IRS website, publications, and tax professionals can all provide useful information about documentation requirements.

Proper record-keeping and documentation are essential for substantiating your deductions and adhering to IRS regulations. You can confidently support your deductions, reduce the risk of errors, and be well-prepared for any potential IRS inquiries or audits by implementing these record-keeping tips and best practices.

Chapter 4: Unlocking Retirement Plan Options for S Corporation Owners

Introduction

Retirement planning is a critical consideration for small business owners, and S corporations offer unique retirement plan options with significant tax advantages. This chapter will delve into the various retirement plans available to S corporation owners, allowing them to make well-informed decisions that are in line with their long-term financial objectives.

Key topics covered in this chapter include:

1. Understanding the importance of retirement planning for small business owners.
2. Exploring retirement plan options available to S corporation owners, including SEP-IRAs, SIMPLE IRAs, 401(k) plans, and defined benefit plans.
3. Eligibility requirements and contribution limits for each type of retirement plan.
4. Comparing the benefits and considerations of different retirement plans.
5. Strategies for maximizing retirement contributions within the confines of S corporation rules.
6. Navigating the fiduciary responsibilities and administrative duties associated with retirement plans.
7. Impact of the Tax Cuts and Jobs Act on retirement plan contributions and withdrawals.
8. Case studies illustrating effective retirement plan strategies for S corporation owners.

By unlocking the potential of retirement plan options, S corporation owners can secure their financial future and enjoy tax advantages that contribute to long-term wealth accumulation and a comfortable retirement.

4.1 Understanding the Importance of Retirement Planning for Small Business Owners

Retirement planning is extremely important for small business owners, and this section aims to highlight the key reasons why it should be a top priority. Small business owners can take proactive steps to secure their financial future by recognizing the importance of retirement planning.

One of the primary reasons retirement planning is so important is the potential difficulties and risks associated with insufficient preparation. Small business owners frequently devote a significant amount of their time, energy, and personal finances to building and growing their companies. However, if they do not plan properly for retirement, they may find themselves unprepared for the future, facing financial difficulties, or being forced to work longer than desired.

Failure to plan for retirement can result in a variety of problems. Small business owners, for example, may struggle to maintain their desired standard of living after retirement if they rely solely on the sale of their businesses for income. Unexpected events, such as health issues or economic downturns, can also disrupt business operations and have a negative impact on retirement savings.

Small business owners can mitigate these risks and protect their financial well-being by planning ahead for retirement. Owners can accumulate wealth over time by establishing retirement savings early on and consistently contributing to retirement accounts. This ensures a comfortable and secure retirement.

Furthermore, retirement planning provides long-term benefits that go beyond financial security. It gives business owners peace of mind by allowing them to focus on the present rather than constantly worrying about the future. Knowing that your retirement needs are being met can reduce stress and allow for a better work-life balance.

Retirement planning also allows small business owners to benefit from tax breaks and incentives. Owners can reduce their current tax liabilities and potentially defer taxes on their contributions and investment gains until retirement by strategically utilizing retirement plans. These tax breaks can have a significant impact on the overall financial picture and help to accumulate long-term wealth.

Furthermore, retirement planning enables small business owners to align their personal goals with those of their company. It encourages them to imagine their ideal retirement lifestyle and create a plan to achieve those goals. Owners can make informed decisions about their businesses and personal finances by setting specific retirement goals and reviewing their progress on a regular basis, ensuring a smooth transition into retirement.

Finally, understanding the significance of retirement planning is critical for small business owners. Owners can secure their financial future by recognizing the potential challenges of inadequate preparation and embracing the long-term benefits of proactive planning. Retirement planning allows you to overcome financial obstacles, achieve peace of mind, maximize tax benefits, and align personal and business goals. Small business owners can pave the way for a rewarding and fulfilling retirement journey with careful consideration and diligent planning.

4.2 Exploring Retirement Plan Options Available to S Corporation Owners

This section provides a thorough overview of retirement plan options tailored specifically to S corporation owners. It intends to familiarize them with the available options, allowing them to make informed decisions that are appropriate for their specific needs and circumstances. SEP-IRAs (Simplified Employee Pension Individual Retirement Accounts), SIMPLE IRAs (Savings Incentive Match Plan for Employees Individual Retirement Accounts), and other retirement plan options available to S corporation owners will be discussed.

1. SEP-IRAs:

The section on SEP-IRAs delves deeply into this retirement plan option. SEP-IRAs enable S corporation owners to contribute to both their own and their employees' retirement accounts. We will go over the requirements for establishing a SEP-IRA, including the requirement that the company have no other qualified retirement plan in place. Furthermore, we will go over SEP-IRA contribution limits, which are generally higher than traditional IRA contribution limits. S corporation owners can evaluate whether this retirement plan aligns with their financial goals by understanding the tax advantages and potential deductions associated with SEP-IRAs. We will also discuss considerations for establishing and managing SEP-IRAs, such as ease of administration and the ability to adjust contributions from year to year.

2. SIMPLE IRAs:

The SIMPLE IRA section emphasizes this alternative retirement plan option available to S corporation owners.

Simple IRAs are intended for small businesses with fewer than 100 employees. We will go over the requirements for S corporation owners to set up a SIMPLE IRA, which include having employees who earned at least $5,000 in compensation in the previous calendar year. We'll look at the contribution limits for SIMPLE IRAs, which allow for both employee salary deferral and employer matching contributions. Understanding the complexities of employer matching contributions is critical for S corporation owners thinking about this retirement plan option. We will also discuss implementation and administration considerations for SIMPLE IRAs, such as the ease of plan setup and simplified reporting requirements.

3. Other Retirement Plan Options:

There are other retirement plan options available to S corporation owners in addition to SEP-IRAs and SIMPLE IRAs. 401(k) plans, individual 401(k) plans, defined benefit plans, and profit-sharing plans are examples of these. I will provide a brief overview of these options, emphasizing their distinguishing features, eligibility requirements, and potential benefits. By investigating these options, S corporation owners can determine whether these retirement plans are compatible with their specific financial goals and the needs of their businesses.

Finally, for effective retirement planning, it is critical to investigate retirement plan options tailored specifically for S corporation owners. Owners can evaluate the features, benefits, and considerations associated with each option by examining SEP-IRAs, SIMPLE IRAs, and other available retirement plans. This knowledge enables S corporation owners to choose the retirement plan that best meets their financial objectives, ensures compliance with IRS regulations, and provides long-term financial security for themselves and their employees.

4.3 Assessing the Benefits and Drawbacks of Different Retirement Plan Options

This section will provide a comparison of the various retirement plan options available to S corporation owners. Our goal is to outline the benefits and drawbacks of each plan, allowing S corporation owners to make informed decisions based on their specific needs and circumstances. We will evaluate the pros and cons of each retirement plan option by taking into account a variety of factors such as contribution limits, administrative complexity, employee participation requirements, and tax implications.

1. **Contribution Limits:**

   The contribution limits imposed by each plan are an important factor to consider when evaluating retirement plans. Higher contribution limits are available in some plans, such as SEP-IRAs and 401(k) plans, allowing for more substantial retirement savings. SIMPLE IRAs, on the other hand, have lower contribution limits but provide the benefit of both employer matching contributions and employee salary deferral contributions. Understanding each plan's contribution limits is critical in determining the maximum amount that can be contributed annually.

2. **Administrative Complexity:**

   The administrative complexity involved in managing and maintaining each retirement plan is another factor to consider. Some plans, such as SEP-IRAs and SIMPLE IRAs, have few administrative requirements, making them relatively simple to set up and maintain. Other alternatives, such as 401(k) plans and defined benefit plans, may necessitate more complex administrative tasks, such as annual testing and reporting. Owners of S corporations should consider their willingness and ability to handle the administrative responsibilities that come with each plan option.

3. **Employee Participation Requirements:**

Certain retirement plans have specific employee participation requirements. SEP-IRAs, for example, allow contributions only from the employer, whereas SIMPLE IRAs require employer matching contributions in addition to employee salary deferral contributions. Other plans, such as 401(k)s, may necessitate greater employee participation. Owners of S corporations should consider the impact of these participation requirements on their business and the level of employee involvement desired.

4. **Tax Implications:**

The tax implications of each retirement plan option should be carefully considered as well. SEP-IRAs and SIMPLE IRAs provide tax benefits by allowing contributions to grow tax-free until withdrawal. Pre-tax and Roth contribution options are available in 401(k) plans, giving participants flexibility in managing their tax liabilities. S corporation owners should consider the tax benefits and consequences of each plan option in light of their personal tax situation and long-term financial goals.

S corporation owners can make informed decisions based on their specific needs by weighing the benefits and drawbacks of various retirement plan options. Contribution limits, administrative complexity, employee participation requirements, and tax implications all play a role in determining the best retirement plan. S corporation owners must carefully consider these factors and, if necessary, seek professional advice to ensure that their chosen retirement plan aligns with their financial goals and supports a secure retirement for themselves and their employees.

4.4 Increasing Contributions and Tax Benefits

In this section, we will look at strategies for increasing contributions and maximizing the tax benefits provided by S corporation retirement plans. These strategies aim to maximize retirement savings while minimizing S corporation owners' tax liabilities. S corporation owners can take full advantage of the available contribution opportunities and maximize the tax benefits associated with their retirement plans by implementing these techniques.

1. **Catch-up Contributions:**

   Using catch-up contributions is an effective strategy for increasing retirement savings. Catch-up contributions allow individuals 50 and older to contribute to their retirement accounts in excess of the standard contribution limits. S corporation owners can accelerate their retirement savings in the years leading up to retirement by taking advantage of catch-up contributions, allowing them to bridge the gap and build a more secure financial future.

2. **Profit-Sharing Contributions:**

   Leveraging profit-sharing contributions is another effective strategy for increasing contributions. S corporation owners can contribute a portion of the company's profits to their retirement plans in the form of profit-sharing contributions. These contributions are distinct from salary deferral contributions, and they can be calculated using a percentage of profits or a predetermined formula. S corporation owners can increase their retirement savings while potentially benefiting from tax breaks by implementing an effective profit-sharing strategy.

3. Contributions through Salary Deferrals:

S corporation owners who choose retirement plans such as 401(k) plans can also maximize their contributions through salary deferrals. Owners can contribute a portion of their income to their retirement accounts on a pre-tax or Roth basis through salary deferral contributions. S corporation owners can increase their retirement savings while lowering their taxable income by contributing a higher percentage of their salary.

4. Matching Contributions:

Where employer matching contributions are required in plans such as SIMPLE IRAs, S corporation owners should consider maximizing the matching contributions. Owners can motivate employees to contribute more to their retirement accounts by offering a generous matching percentage, increasing overall retirement savings for both the owner and the employees. This not only aids in recruitment and retention efforts, but also maximizes the tax benefits of the retirement plan.

5. Annual Contribution Assessments:

It is critical for S corporation owners to assess their contribution levels on a regular basis to ensure they are maximizing their retirement savings within the IRS limits. Owners can take full advantage of available contribution opportunities by reviewing and adjusting their contributions on an annual basis, taking into account factors such as business profitability, personal financial goals, and tax considerations.

S corporation owners can maximize their retirement contributions while taking advantage of the tax advantages provided by their chosen retirement plans by implementing these strategies. To determine the most appropriate strategies based on individual circumstances and to ensure compliance with IRS regulations, it is critical to consult with a financial advisor or tax professional. S corporation owners will be able to maximize their retirement savings and improve their long-term financial security through proactive planning and periodic assessments.

4.5 Compliance and Reporting Requirements

When establishing and managing retirement plans for S corporation owners, it is critical to ensure compliance with IRS regulations. This section will provide an overview of the S corporation's retirement plan compliance and reporting requirements. Understanding these obligations will assist S corporation owners in carrying out their duties and mitigating potential risks.

1. **Annual Filing Obligations:**

   To remain in compliance with IRS regulations, S corporation owners must fulfill certain annual filing obligations. These requirements will differ depending on the type of retirement plan selected. SEP-IRAs, for example, do not generally require a separate annual filing, whereas 401(k) plans and SIMPLE IRAs may require annual Form 5500 or Form 5500-EZ filings. To avoid penalties or non-compliance issues, S corporation owners must stay informed about their specific filing obligations and deadlines.

2. **Employee Disclosures:**

When implementing a retirement plan, S corporation owners must provide certain disclosures to employees. The plan, eligibility requirements, contribution limits, vesting schedules, and investment options are typically included in these disclosures. It is critical to communicate these details in a timely and accurate manner to ensure that employees are well-informed about their participation in the retirement plan. Owners of S corporations should develop a process for providing these disclosures to employees and keep records to demonstrate compliance with these requirements.

3. **Best Documentation Practices:**

Maintaining accurate and comprehensive documentation is critical for IRS compliance. To substantiate the establishment, contributions, and operation of the retirement plan, S corporation owners should establish rigorous record-keeping practices. Plan documents, adoption agreements, employee communications, contribution records, investment statements, and any plan amendments should all be included in this documentation. S corporation owners can demonstrate compliance, effectively respond to IRS inquiries, and support their filings and deductions during an audit by implementing proper documentation practices.

4. **Monitoring Plan Operations:**

   To ensure ongoing compliance, S corporation owners should regularly monitor the operations of their retirement plan. Overseeing contributions, ensuring timely deposit of employee deferrals, monitoring vesting schedules, and reviewing investment performance are all part of the job. Regular plan reviews and internal audits can aid in identifying any issues with compliance or areas for improvement. In addition, hiring a third-party administrator or a qualified retirement plan professional can provide expertise and assistance in ensuring ongoing regulatory compliance.

5. **Educational Efforts:**

   It is critical for S corporation owners to keep up with the changing retirement plan landscape and stay informed about regulatory changes. To stay current on compliance requirements, it is critical to invest in ongoing education and seek professional advice. Attending seminars, webinars, or workshops, as well as engaging with retirement plan experts who can provide valuable insights and guidance tailored to the specific needs of S corporation owners, can help achieve this.

S corporation owners can ensure that their retirement plans operate in accordance with IRS guidelines by understanding and adhering to compliance and reporting requirements. This will help to reduce the risk of penalties, maintain employee trust, and lay the groundwork for long-term retirement planning. To ensure compliance and navigate the complex landscape of retirement plan regulations, it is recommended that you consult with a qualified retirement plan professional or tax advisor.

4.6 Considering Additional Retirement Planning Options

S corporation owners have access to a variety of alternative retirement planning options in addition to the traditional retirement plans discussed previously. This section will look into these extra options and give you an overview of their features, benefits, and considerations. S corporation owners can evaluate which retirement plan best aligns with their specific goals and financial circumstances by considering these options.

1. **Individual 401(k) Plans:**

   Individual 401(k) plans, also known as solo 401(k) plans, are intended for self-employed individuals and business owners who do not employ anyone other than their spouse. When compared to SEP-IRAs and SIMPLE IRAs, these plans have higher contribution limits. Individual 401(k) plans may be advantageous for S corporation owners who want to contribute more to their retirement savings. This section will go over the eligibility requirements, contribution limits, employer and employee contributions, loan provisions, and administrative requirements for individual 401(k) plans.

2. **Defined Benefit Plans:**

   Another retirement planning option for S corporation owners is defined benefit plans. These plans, also known as pension plans, offer a fixed retirement benefit based on factors such as salary history and years of service. While defined benefit plans necessitate actuarial calculations and may incur additional administrative costs, they provide the opportunity for significant retirement savings. This section will look at the characteristics, contribution limits, funding requirements, and complexities of defined benefit plans.

3. **Roth IRAs:**

   When compared to traditional retirement plans, Roth IRAs provide distinct tax advantages. Contributions to Roth IRAs are made after-tax dollars, but qualified distributions are tax-free in retirement. This can be especially beneficial for S corporation owners who expect to be in a higher tax bracket during retirement. This section will go over the eligibility requirements, contribution limits, tax advantages, and factors to consider when incorporating Roth IRAs into an overall retirement plan strategy.

4. **Considerations and Evaluations:**

   S corporation owners should carefully evaluate their specific needs, financial situation, and long-term retirement goals when considering additional retirement planning options. Contribution flexibility, tax planning objectives, investment preferences, administrative complexity, and the potential impact on employees should all be considered. Seeking advice from a qualified retirement planning professional or tax advisor can provide useful insights and assist S corporation owners in making informed decisions about these alternative retirement planning options.

S corporation owners can broaden their retirement savings strategies and tailor their plans to best meet their unique circumstances by investigating additional retirement planning options. Each option has its own set of benefits and drawbacks, so it's critical to weigh these options against your personal objectives and consult with professionals who can provide specialized advice. Choosing the best retirement plan will assist S corporation owners in achieving their retirement goals and maximizing their financial security in the future.

Conclusion

This chapter has emphasized the importance of retirement planning for S corporation owners and provided an in-depth examination of the retirement plan options available to them. S corporation owners can take proactive steps to secure their financial future by recognizing the importance of retirement planning.

It is critical to understand the various retirement plan options discussed in this chapter in order to make informed decisions. S corporation owners can select and implement retirement plans that align with their long-term needs by weighing the benefits and drawbacks of each plan, considering individual financial goals, and weighing factors such as contribution limits, administrative complexity, employee participation requirements, and tax implications.

SEP-IRAs, SIMPLE IRAs, individual 401(k) plans, defined benefit plans, and Roth IRAs have all been discussed in this chapter. Each option has unique features and benefits, allowing S corporation owners to tailor their retirement strategies to their specific circumstances and goals.

Additionally, compliance with IRS regulations and reporting requirements is critical to the successful implementation and administration of retirement plans. S corporation owners can avoid potential penalties and protect the integrity of their retirement plans by following these guidelines.

Finally, S corporation owners are encouraged to take retirement planning seriously and to take advantage of the available retirement plan options in order to secure their financial future. They can make educated choices that align with their unique circumstances and aspirations if they understand the benefits, limitations, and considerations associated with each plan. Seeking professional advice from retirement planning experts or tax advisors can help you make better decisions and provide valuable insights.

S corporation owners can pave the way for a financially secure and comfortable retirement by embracing retirement planning and selecting appropriate retirement plans, allowing them to enjoy the fruits of their labor while achieving their long-term goals.

Chapter 5: Managing S Corporation Shareholder Basis

Introduction

In this chapter, we will look at how to manage shareholder basis for S corporation owners. Understanding and effectively managing shareholder basis is critical for tax planning and IRS compliance. This chapter delves deeply into the concept of shareholder basis, its importance in S corporation taxation, and strategies for maximizing tax benefits through effective basis management.

Key topics covered in this chapter include:

1. The concept of shareholder basis and its importance in S corporation taxation.
2. Determining initial shareholder basis and adjustments over time.
3. Impact of distributions, loans, and contributions on shareholder basis.
4. Strategies for increasing shareholder basis to facilitate tax-free distributions and avoid negative tax consequences.
5. Managing shareholder loans and their impact on basis calculations.
6. Tracking basis limitations and ensuring compliance with IRS rules.
7. Real-world examples illustrating the practical application of managing shareholder basis.
8. Importance of accurate record-keeping and documentation for shareholder basis calculations.

S corporation owners can unlock additional tax planning opportunities and optimize their overall tax position within the S corporation structure by mastering the complexities of managing shareholder basis. Understanding the concepts, strategies, and compliance requirements discussed in this chapter will enable S corporation owners to make informed decisions, maximize tax benefits, and ensure IRS compliance.

5.1 The Concept of Shareholder Basis and Its Importance in S Corporation Taxation

This section provides an in-depth explanation of the concept of shareholder basis and its importance in S corporation taxation. Understanding shareholder basis is critical for determining the tax implications of S corporation operations and ensuring tax compliance.

The financial investment or capital that a shareholder has in their S corporation is referred to as the shareholder basis. It is used to assess the extent to which a shareholder receives a tax-free return of capital, the deductibility of losses, and the taxability of distributions.

Maintaining an accurate and up-to-date basis is critical for proper reporting and tax compliance. It enables S corporation owners to accurately track the tax implications of their company's financial activities. A thorough understanding of shareholder basis enables owners to make informed decisions about distributions, contributions, and other transactions, ensuring they comply with the Internal Revenue Service's (IRS) tax rules and guidelines.

Accurate basis calculations are critical in many aspects of S corporation taxation. It has an impact on how income, losses, distributions, and contributions are treated. Shareholders must understand their basis in order to accurately report their taxable income, claim appropriate deductions, and determine the tax consequences of S corporation distributions.

S corporation owners can avoid potential errors or misinterpretations that could lead to noncompliance with tax regulations and potential penalties by keeping their records accurate and up to date. It enables owners to strategically manage their financial activities and optimize their tax positions within the S corporation structure, allowing for proper tax planning.

To summarize, S corporation owners must understand the concept of shareholder basis in order to navigate the complexities of taxation. It is crucial in determining the tax implications of S corporation operations, such as the taxability of distributions and the deductibility of losses. Owners can ensure proper reporting, compliance with tax regulations, and informed decisions to maximize tax benefits within the S corporation structure by maintaining an accurate and up-to-date basis.

5.2 Establishing the Initial Shareholder Basis and Making Adjustments Over Time

This section focuses on the process of determining the initial shareholder basis and any subsequent adjustments. Accurately calculating the initial shareholder basis and tracking subsequent adjustments are critical for managing and maximizing the tax advantages of the S corporation structure.

Typically, the initial shareholder basis is established at the time the shareholder invests in the S corporation. It represents the shareholder's initial capital contribution and serves as the starting point for basis calculations. This initial investment, which can be either cash or property, serves as the foundation for determining the shareholder's tax position within the S corporation.

Adjustments to the shareholder basis may occur as the S corporation operates and engages in various financial activities. These adjustments reflect changes in the shareholder's investment and the S corporation's overall financial position. Common adjustments include shareholder contributions, income allocations, losses incurred, and distributions received.

Contributions made by shareholders, such as additional investments or loans to the S corporation, raise the basis. These contributions can take the form of cash, property, or a liability assumption. Shareholders can ensure that their basis is adjusted to reflect the increased investment in the company by accurately tracking these contributions.

The S corporation's income allocations and losses have an impact on the shareholder basis. The allocation of taxable income raises the basis, while the allocation of losses lowers it. Shareholders must keep accurate track of these adjustments in order to calculate their basis and determine the tax implications of these income or loss allocations.

Distributions received by shareholders from the S corporation also have an impact on the basis. Distributions are generally tax-free to the extent of the shareholder's basis. Distributions that exceed the shareholder's basis, on the other hand, may result in taxable income. It is critical to track and adjust the basis for distributions received in order to determine the taxability of these distributions.

Understanding and correctly calculating these shareholder basis adjustments is critical for accurate tax reporting and compliance. It enables S corporation owners to calculate the tax implications of a variety of financial transactions, such as contributions, income allocations, losses, and distributions. Shareholders can ensure the accuracy of their basis calculations and optimize their tax positions within the S corporation structure by diligently tracking and managing these adjustments over time.

In conclusion, determining the initial shareholder basis and tracking the changes over time are critical for managing the tax implications within the S corporation. Accurate basis calculations allow shareholders to make informed decisions, report their taxable income correctly, and determine the tax implications of distributions. Shareholders can effectively manage their basis and maximize their tax benefits within the S corporation structure by understanding and diligently tracking these adjustments.

5.3 Impact of Distributions, Loans, and Contributions on Shareholder Basis

This section delves into the impact of S corporation distributions, loans, and contributions on the shareholder basis. Understanding how these financial transactions affect basis calculations is critical for maintaining accurate basis tracking and management.

Distributions from an S corporation can affect the shareholder basis differently depending on whether they are taxable or tax-free. Dividends, which are taxable distributions, do not generally affect the shareholder basis. These distributions are typically regarded as a return on investment by the shareholder and are subject to dividend taxation. Shareholders should be aware that taxable distributions have no effect on their basis.

Tax-free distributions, on the other hand, can have a significant impact on the shareholder basis. A distribution is considered tax-free if it does not exceed the shareholder's basis. These distributions reduce the basis and represent a return on investment for the shareholder without incurring additional tax liability. It is critical to accurately track tax-free distributions in order to properly adjust the basis to reflect the reduction.

Another factor influencing the basis is shareholder loans to the S corporation. A shareholder's loan to the corporation has no direct impact on the basis. However, the loan might have tax repercussions, such as the shareholder earning interest income. For tax purposes, it is critical to properly document and track shareholder loans and separate them from capital contributions.

Shareholder contributions, whether in cash, property, or the assumption of liabilities, increase the basis. These contributions are new investments in the S corporation that increase the shareholder's stake in the company. It is critical to accurately record and track these contributions in order to ensure that the basis is adjusted and reflects the increased investment.

Understanding the impact of distributions, loans, and contributions on shareholder basis enables S corporation owners to make informed decisions and track their basis accurately. Dividends can be properly adjusted and negative tax consequences avoided by distinguishing between taxable and tax-free distributions. Similarly, accurately documenting shareholder loans and contributions aids in maintaining an accurate basis and ensures tax compliance.

In summary, distributions, loans, and contributions all have different effects on a S corporation's shareholder basis. Taxable distributions have no effect on the basis, whereas tax-free distributions do. Shareholder loans have indirect tax consequences, while contributions raise the basis. Shareholders can effectively manage their basis and make informed decisions about their S corporation's financial activities by understanding these impacts and diligently tracking these transactions.

5.4 Strategies for Increasing Shareholder Basis to Facilitate Tax-Free Distributions and Avoid Negative Tax Consequences

This section looks at how S corporation owners can use strategic approaches to increase shareholder basis, allowing for tax-free distributions and mitigating potential negative tax consequences. Owners can optimize their tax planning and reap the benefits of S corporation taxation by proactively managing basis.

Making additional capital contributions to the S corporation is one effective strategy for increasing shareholder basis. By injecting more funds into the company, shareholders increase their investment and, thus, their basis. These capital contributions, which can be made in cash, property, or by assuming liabilities, directly increase the basis. To ensure accurate basis calculations, these contributions must be properly documented and recorded.

Another strategy is to distribute losses to shareholders. S corporations pass their losses through to shareholders, who can deduct their allocated share of the losses on their personal tax returns. This deduction can lower a shareholder's taxable income while increasing their basis. By actively allocating losses to shareholders, they can increase their basis and potentially create opportunities for future tax-free distributions. It is critical to follow the allocation rules of the S corporation and keep proper documentation of the allocated losses.

Another effective strategy for increasing shareholder basis is to keep income within the S corporation. When an S corporation keeps its earnings rather than distributing them to shareholders, the accumulated income increases the shareholders' basis. Retained earnings reflect the shareholder's proportionate share of the company's accumulated profits, which raises the basis of the shares. Shareholders can build their basis over time by retaining income within the corporation, providing a stronger foundation for tax planning and potential tax-free distributions.

It is critical for S corporation owners to evaluate and implement these strategies with care and knowledge. Owners can determine the most appropriate approach to increasing basis by assessing the specific needs and goals of the business. Working closely with a tax professional is recommended to ensure compliance with tax regulations and the development of a comprehensive plan tailored to the S corporation's specific circumstances.

S corporation owners can facilitate tax-free distributions and minimize negative tax consequences by strategically increasing shareholder basis through capital contributions, allocating losses, and retaining income. To ensure compliance and maximize tax planning opportunities, it is critical to consider the unique factors and limitations of each strategy and consult with a tax advisor.

In summary, using strategies to increase shareholder basis allows S corporation owners to make tax-free distributions while mitigating negative tax consequences. Owners can effectively manage their basis and optimize their tax planning by making additional capital contributions, allocating losses, and retaining income within the corporation. Proactive basis management is a valuable tool for maximizing tax benefits and supporting S corporation owners' long-term financial goals.

5.5 Shareholder Loan Management and the Effect on Basis Calculations

This section delves into the management of shareholder loans and the significance of their impact on S-corporation basis calculations.

It emphasizes the rules and considerations pertaining to shareholder loans to or from the S corporation, emphasizing the importance of proper documentation and adherence to IRS guidelines.

Shareholder loans can have an impact on S corporation basis calculations. When a shareholder lends money to the corporation, it has no effect on their basis. The loan amount is considered a debt obligation that the corporation owes to the shareholder, and it has no bearing on the shareholder's basis.

In contrast, when an S corporation lends money to a shareholder, it does not reduce the shareholder's basis. The loan is treated as a debt obligation owed to the corporation by the shareholder, and it has no effect on the shareholder's basis in the company.

To ensure clarity and compliance, shareholder loans must be properly documented. A formal loan agreement should clearly outline the loan's terms, including the repayment schedule, interest rate, and any applicable collateral. Both the shareholder and the corporation can maintain a clear understanding of the debt obligation and its impact on basis calculations by properly documenting the loan.

Furthermore, when managing shareholder loans, it is critical to follow IRS guidelines. The loan must be structured as a legitimate debt with a reasonable expectation of repayment. If the IRS determines that a shareholder loan is a disguised distribution or contribution rather than a legitimate debt, it may disregard the loan for basis purposes and treat it as a taxable event. As a result, it is critical to ensure that the loan adheres to established commercial lending practices and has a genuine repayment intent.

When managing shareholder loans, accurate record-keeping is essential. The S corporation should keep detailed loan documentation, including records of loan disbursements, repayments, and any accrued interest. In the event of an IRS audit, both the shareholder and the corporation should keep accurate records to substantiate the existence and terms of the loan.

S corporation owners can maintain accurate basis calculations and avoid potential tax issues by carefully managing shareholder loans and adhering to IRS guidelines. Working with a tax professional is recommended to ensure loan documentation compliance and to navigate any complexities associated with shareholder loans.

To summarize, managing shareholder loans necessitates meticulous attention to detail and adherence to IRS regulations. Understanding how loans affect basis calculations and keeping proper documentation are essential for accurate reporting and compliance. S corporation owners can ensure the integrity of basis calculations and reduce the risk of tax-related complications by effectively managing shareholder loans.

5.6 Monitoring Basis Limitations and Ensuring IRS Compliance

This section focuses on basis limitations and their significance in determining the deductibility of losses and the taxability of S corporation distributions. We go over the IRS's rules and thresholds, emphasizing the importance of diligently tracking and managing basis limitations in order to stay in compliance.

Basis limitations are important in S corporation taxation, particularly when it comes to the deductibility of losses and the taxability of distributions. An S corporation shareholder's basis determines whether losses can be claimed on their personal tax return and whether distributions from the corporation are taxable or tax-free.

The IRS establishes rules and thresholds for basis limitations, which shareholders must follow. A shareholder's adjusted basis in S corporation stock is what primarily determines these restrictions. To ensure compliance with these rules, it is critical that you track and maintain accurate records of your basis as a shareholder.

When an S corporation suffers a loss, shareholders can deduct the loss on their personal tax return only to the extent of their stock basis. If the loss exceeds the basis of the shareholder, it may be limited or suspended until there is enough basis to absorb the loss. As a result, accurately tracking basis is critical to maximizing loss deductibility and minimizing any limitations.

In a similar vein, when the S corporation distributes money to shareholders, the shareholder's basis determines whether or not those distributions are taxable. Distributions are tax-free up to the shareholder's basis in the stock. Distributions that exceed the basis may be taxable and subject to capital gains tax. Monitoring basis limitations is therefore critical to ensuring proper reporting and avoiding unexpected tax liabilities.

To effectively track basis limitations, shareholders should keep detailed records of their initial basis and any subsequent adjustments, including contributions, distributions, and other relevant transactions. It is critical to keep meticulous records of basis increases and decreases in order to calculate the remaining basis available for deducting losses or receiving tax-free distributions.

Proactively managing basis limitations necessitates regular monitoring and consideration of a variety of factors, including the allocation of income and losses among shareholders, stock purchases or sales, and any other events that affect basis. Shareholders can ensure compliance with IRS rules and maximize tax benefits by remaining vigilant and keeping accurate records.

Finally, tracking basis limitations is critical for S corporation shareholders in determining the taxability of distributions and the deductibility of losses. Following IRS rules and thresholds, as well as maintaining meticulous basis records, enables shareholders to accurately report their tax obligations and maximize available tax benefits. S corporation owners can effectively navigate the complexities of basis limitations and make informed tax planning decisions by staying informed and in compliance.

5.7 Real-World Examples Illustrating the Practical Application of Shareholder Basis Management

In this section, we present real-world examples that demonstrate how to manage shareholder basis in practice. These examples are intended to give readers valuable insight into how basis calculations and adjustments work in various scenarios and how they affect tax planning strategies.

Example 1: John is a S corporation shareholder who made an initial $50,000 investment in the company. He has received $20,000 in distributions and has allocated $10,000 in losses over the years. To calculate John's current basis, we must take into account his initial investment, distributions, and allocated losses.

John's starting point is $50,000.
-$20,000 in distributions received
Losses allocated: -$10,000

John's current basis would be calculated as follows, based on these figures:
$50,000 - $20,000 - $10,000 = $20,000

This example shows how distributions and losses affect the shareholder basis. John can accurately determine his remaining basis by tracking these transactions, which affect the taxability of future distributions and the deductibility of losses.

Example 2: Sarah, another S corporation shareholder, decides to increase her basis by making an additional capital contribution of $15,000. She also receives a $5,000 distribution from the company. To determine Sarah's new basis, we must take into account her existing basis, capital contribution, and distribution.

Sarah's current basis is $30,000
+$15,000 in capital contribution
-$5,000 in distribution received

We would perform the following calculation to determine Sarah's updated basis:

$30,000 + $15,000 - $5,000 = $40,000

This example shows how shareholder contributions can increase basis, potentially allowing for future tax-free distributions. Shareholders can increase their basis and optimize their tax planning by actively managing and strategically making contributions.

These real-world examples demonstrate how to manage the shareholder basis and how it affects tax planning strategies. Shareholders can gain a better understanding of how basis calculations work in practice by considering various scenarios and transactions. This knowledge enables them to make educated decisions about optimizing their basis, maximizing tax benefits, and adhering to IRS regulations.

It is important to note that these examples are merely illustrative and may not cover all possible scenarios. Each shareholder's situation will be different, so it is best to consult with a qualified tax professional to determine the specific implications and requirements based on individual circumstances.

S corporation owners can develop a deeper understanding of managing shareholder basis and effectively apply this knowledge to their own tax planning strategies by studying these real-world examples and seeking professional guidance.

5.8 The Importance of Correct Record-Keeping and Documentation in Shareholder Basis Calculations

In this section, we emphasize the importance of accurate record-keeping and documentation in effectively managing shareholder basis. Maintaining detailed records, documenting transactions, and organizing supporting documents are critical for accurate basis calculations and ensuring IRS compliance.

Accurate record-keeping is the foundation for effective shareholder management. Shareholders can accurately calculate their basis by keeping track of all relevant transactions, such as initial investments, contributions, distributions, and allocated losses. Detailed records provide a clear audit trail and allow shareholders to justify their basis calculations if necessary.

Documentation is also essential in supporting basis calculations and adhering to IRS regulations. It is critical to keep records that validate the occurrence and nature of transactions. Investment agreements, capital contribution records, distribution statements, loan agreements, and any other relevant financial records are examples of such documents.

It is critical to organize supporting documents in a systematic manner for efficient record-keeping and easy retrieval when needed. To keep a well-organized record-keeping system, you can use electronic storage systems or physical file organization methods. Shareholders can quickly access the necessary information during basis calculations or when responding to IRS inquiries by categorizing and labeling documents appropriately.

Accurate record-keeping and documentation provide several advantages. They ensure the dependability and accuracy of basis calculations, reducing the possibility of errors or discrepancies. Furthermore, well-organized records provide transparency and demonstrate compliance with IRS guidelines, which increases the credibility of basis calculations.

Furthermore, comprehensive records and supporting documents serve as evidence to substantiate basis calculations and transactions in the event of an IRS audit or examination. They provide a solid foundation for defending reported basis accuracy and mitigating potential penalties or IRS disputes.

Consider the following best practices for maintaining accurate record-keeping and documentation for shareholder-basis calculations:

1. Record all relevant transactions, including investments, contributions, distributions, and allocated losses, as soon as possible.
2. Maintain duplicates of investment agreements, capital contribution records, distribution statements, loan agreements, and other relevant documents.
3. Using clear labels and categories, organize documents in a systematic manner, either electronically or in physical files.
4. Review and update records on a regular basis to ensure they are complete, accurate, and up to date.
5. To protect against loss or damage, keep records in a secure location and back up electronic files.

By following these practices, S corporation owners can maintain accurate and reliable basis calculations, demonstrate compliance with IRS regulations, and confidently navigate the complexities of managing shareholder basis.

Remember that the information provided here is for educational purposes only, and it is best to seek personalized advice and guidance from a qualified tax professional or accountant regarding specific record-keeping practices and IRS requirements.

Conclusion

Understanding the complexities of managing shareholder basis is critical for S corporation owners seeking to maximize their overall tax position within the S corporation structure. S corporation owners can make informed decisions, maximize tax benefits, and ensure IRS compliance by understanding the concepts, strategies, and compliance requirements discussed in this chapter.

Managing shareholder basis enables S corporation owners to effectively navigate the complexities of tax planning. Owners can determine the tax consequences of S corporation operations, including the deductibility of losses and the taxability of distributions, by accurately calculating and tracking basis. This understanding enables them to plan their business activities strategically and reduce their tax liabilities.

We have covered key topics related to managing shareholder basis throughout this chapter. We talked about shareholder basis and its significance in S corporation taxation, emphasizing the importance of accurate basis calculations for proper reporting and compliance with tax regulations.

We also discussed how to determine the initial shareholder basis and the various adjustments that may occur over time, such as investments, contributions, income, losses, and distributions. Understanding these adjustments is critical for maintaining an accurate basis and managing tax planning strategies effectively.

We also looked at the impact of distributions, loans, and contributions on a per-share basis. Differentiating between taxable and tax-free distributions, as well as considering the treatment of shareholder loans and contributions, is critical for accurate basis calculations and ensuring IRS compliance.

Strategies for increasing shareholder basis, such as making additional capital contributions, allocating losses, and retaining income within the S corporation, were also discussed. S corporation owners can facilitate tax-free distributions and reduce the risk of negative tax consequences by proactively managing basis.

Furthermore, we investigated the management of shareholder loans and their effect on basis calculations. When dealing with loans made to or from the S corporation by shareholders, it is critical to follow proper documentation and IRS guidelines.

Furthermore, we emphasized the importance of tracking basis limitations and ensuring compliance with IRS rules. Understanding the IRS's rules and thresholds is critical for determining loss deductibility and distribution taxability.

Real-world examples were provided to demonstrate how to manage shareholder basis in various scenarios. These examples shed light on how basis calculations and adjustments work in practice, as well as how they affect tax planning strategies.

Finally, we emphasized the importance of maintaining accurate records and documentation for shareholder basis calculations. Maintaining detailed records, documenting transactions, and organizing supporting documents are critical for accurate basis calculations, meeting IRS requirements, and providing a solid foundation in the event of an IRS audit or examination.

S corporation owners can optimize their tax planning, unlock additional tax benefits, and ensure adherence to IRS regulations by mastering the concepts, strategies, and compliance requirements covered in this chapter.

It is important to note that the information in this chapter is provided solely for educational purposes. S corporation owners should seek personalized advice and guidance from a qualified tax professional or accountant regarding their specific situation, as well as ensure compliance with current tax laws and regulations.

Chapter 6: Taking Advantage of the Qualified Business Income Deduction

Introduction

The Tax Cuts and Jobs Act's Qualified Business Income (QBI) deduction has proven to be a valuable tax-saving opportunity for S corporation owners. The purpose of the QBI deduction, eligibility requirements, calculation methods, limitations, and strategies for maximizing its benefits are all covered in this chapter. S corporation owners can reduce their tax liability and keep more of their hard-earned income by understanding and utilizing the QBI deduction.

Key topics covered in this chapter include:

1. Overview of the Qualified Business Income deduction and its purpose.
2. Eligibility criteria for S corporation owners to qualify for the deduction.
3. Calculating the QBI deduction and understanding the limitations and phase-out thresholds.
4. Strategies to maximize the QBI deduction through optimizing salary, deductions, and business structure.
5. Interaction of the QBI deduction with other tax provisions and deductions.
6. Real-life scenarios demonstrating the impact of the QBI deduction on tax savings.
7. Updates and changes to the QBI deduction rules and regulations.
8. Tips for accurate reporting and documentation to support the QBI deduction.

S corporation owners can significantly reduce their taxable income and keep more of their hard-earned money by taking advantage of the Qualified Business Income deduction. However, it is important to note that the information in this chapter is provided solely for educational purposes. S corporation owners should seek personalized advice and guidance from a qualified tax professional or accountant.

6.1 Purpose and Overview of the Qualified Business Income Deduction

This section provides an in-depth examination of the Qualified Business Income (QBI) deduction, shedding light on its purpose and the intended benefits it provides to S corporation owners. The QBI deduction is a tax provision designed to provide tax relief while also encouraging small business growth and investment.

Pass-through entities like S corporations that generate qualified business income can deduct up to 20% of it from eligible taxpayers' taxes. It was included in the Tax Cuts and Jobs Act to provide tax breaks while also encouraging the growth of small businesses, which are critical contributors to the economy.

Reduced effective tax rates on income from pass-through entities is the main objective of the QBI deduction. S corporation owners can retain more of their earnings by allowing a portion of qualified business income to be deducted, stimulating business growth and investment opportunities.

The QBI deduction encourages entrepreneurs to start and grow their businesses, promoting innovation, job creation, and economic development. It recognizes the important role that small businesses play in driving the economy and seeks to reduce their tax burden, allowing them to reinvest in their operations, hire more employees, and give back to their communities.

The QBI deduction encourages business owners to reinvest profits in equipment, research and development, marketing initiatives, and employee training by lowering S corporation owners' tax liability. This reinvestment has the potential to boost productivity, competitiveness, and long-term viability.

Furthermore, by aligning the tax treatment of pass-through entities with that of traditional corporations, which benefit from lower tax rates, the QBI deduction promotes fairness. Its goal is to level the playing field and allow S corporation owners to compete on an equal footing in the business landscape.

Overall, the QBI deduction is a valuable tax-saving opportunity for S corporation owners, allowing them to keep a larger portion of their business income. The deduction promotes economic prosperity by encouraging business growth and investment and rewarding the entrepreneurial spirit that propels small businesses forward.

While this section provides an overview of the QBI deduction, specific eligibility criteria, calculations, and limitations will be discussed further in subsequent sections of this chapter. To understand the complexities of the QBI deduction and how it applies to their specific circumstances, S corporation owners should consult with a qualified tax professional or accountant.

6.2 Eligibility Criteria for S Corporation Owners to Qualify for the Deduction

In this section, we look at the requirements that S corporation owners must meet in order to be eligible for the Qualified Business Income (QBI) deduction. These criteria include a variety of factors, such as the type of business, taxable income thresholds, and restrictions on specified service trades or businesses (SSTBs). Understanding these criteria is critical for determining eligibility and maximizing the QBI deduction's benefits.

S corporation owners must operate a qualified trade or business to be eligible for the QBI deduction. With certain exceptions, such as performing services as an employee, the term "qualified trade or business" generally includes any trade or business conducted within the United States. The majority of businesses, including professional services, manufacturing, retail, and consulting, are classified as qualified trades or businesses. However, as discussed below, certain specified service trades or businesses (SSTBs) may face additional restrictions.

1. **Taxable Income Limits:**

   The QBI deduction is subject to taxable income limits. For the tax year 2023, the thresholds are $329,800 for married couples filing jointly and $164,925 for single filers or married couples filing separately. If the taxpayer's taxable income is less than these amounts, they are generally eligible for the full 20% QBI deduction. However, if the taxable income exceeds the thresholds, the deduction may be limited or phased out.

2. SSTBs (Specified Service Trades or Businesses):

SSTBs are specific types of businesses that face additional restrictions on the QBI deduction. Professions such as law, accounting, health, consulting, athletics, and financial services are examples of SSTBs. The QBI deduction is phased out for SSTBs as taxable income increases, and it may be completely disallowed above certain income levels. However, it is important to note that the SSTB limitation only applies to taxpayers whose taxable income exceeds the previously mentioned threshold amounts.

3. Limitations on Wages and Capital:

In addition to the thresholds and SSTB limitations, the QBI deduction may also be subject to additional restrictions based on employee wages and the unadjusted basis of qualified property that the business owns. These restrictions are intended to prevent the deduction from being abused and to ensure that it primarily benefits businesses with a large employee payroll and an investment in tangible assets.

Understanding these eligibility criteria is critical for S corporation owners in determining eligibility for the QBI deduction and strategizing ways to maximize its benefits. S corporation owners can position themselves to take full advantage of the QBI deduction by evaluating their business structure, managing taxable income, and considering the impact of any SSTB limitations.

It is critical to seek the advice of a knowledgeable tax professional or accountant who can provide guidance tailored to specific circumstances and assist in navigating the complexities of the eligibility requirements. They can assess eligibility, analyze the business's unique situation, and assist in maximizing the potential benefits of the QBI deduction while ensuring compliance with IRS regulations.

6.3 Calculating the QBI Deduction and Understanding the Limitations and Phase-out Thresholds

In this section, we walk S corporation owners through the process of calculating the Qualified Business Income (QBI) deduction. We explain the components of the calculation, such as qualified business income, W-2 wage and capital limitations, and taxable income phase-out thresholds. Understanding these calculations and limitations is critical for determining the amount of the deduction that S corporation owners can claim accurately.

1. Qualified Business Income (QBI):

Determining qualified business income is the first step in calculating the QBI deduction. The net income generated by qualified trades or businesses operated by the S corporation is referred to as qualified business income. It includes ordinary income and business deductions but excludes certain investment income, capital gains, and losses.

2. W-2 Wage and Capital Limitations:

After determining the QBI, S corporation owners must consider the W-2 wage and capital limitations. These restrictions are in place to ensure that the QBI deduction benefits businesses with a large employee payroll and an investment in tangible assets. The restrictions compare employee wages and the unadjusted basis of qualified property that the business owns to the QBI. The IRS outlines the specific calculations and rules for these limitations, which may necessitate consultation with a tax professional to ensure accurate application.

3. Thresholds for Phase-Out:

The QBI deduction has phase-out thresholds based on taxable income. For the tax year 2023, the thresholds are $329,800 for married couples filing jointly and $164,925 for single filers or married couples filing separately. If your taxable income exceeds these limits, the QBI deduction may be limited or phased out gradually. The IRS determines the specific phase-out rules, which are based on the taxpayer's filing status and income level.

S corporation owners can accurately determine the amount they can claim by understanding the calculation of the QBI deduction. It is important to note that calculating the QBI deduction can be complicated, especially when wage and capital limitations and phase-out thresholds are considered. To ensure accurate calculations and compliance with IRS regulations, it is recommended that you consult with a tax professional or accountant.

Tax professionals can help S corporation owners navigate the complexities of the QBI deduction, determine the eligible amount, and maximize the benefits within the parameters of the tax law. They can also advise on record-keeping requirements and the documentation required to support the QBI deduction calculation.

6.4 Methods for Increasing the QBI Deduction by Optimizing Salary, Deductions, and Business Structure

This section delves into the various strategies that S corporation owners can employ to maximize their Qualified Business Income (QBI) deduction. Owners can effectively increase their deductions and reduce their overall tax liability by implementing these strategies. The key strategies include maximizing allowable deductions, optimizing salary levels, and considering potential changes to the business structure.

1. **Salary Level Optimization:** The salary paid to S corporation owners has an impact on the QBI deduction. The salary should be reasonable and commensurate with the owner's services. Owners can maximize their QBI deduction by striking the right balance between salary and distributions. A higher salary increases the amount of QBI that is eligible, resulting in a larger deduction. However, it is critical to ensure that the salary remains reasonable in order to avoid IRS scrutiny.

2. **Maximizing Allowable Deductions:** S corporation owners should carefully review their business expenses and claim all eligible deductions. Owners can reduce their taxable income and, as a result, increase their QBI deduction by taking advantage of all allowable deductions. This includes qualified business expenses like rent, supplies, advertising, and employee wages. To ensure proper classification and documentation of deductible expenses, consult with a tax professional or accountant.

3. **Consider Potential Business Structure Changes:** In some cases, restructuring the business entity can provide additional opportunities to maximize the QBI deduction. Converting from an S corporation to a different entity type, such as a partnership or sole proprietorship, for example, may result in a higher QBI deduction due to differences in how certain deductions or limitations are treated. Before making any changes to the business structure, however, it is critical to carefully evaluate the potential benefits and consult with a tax professional to assess the overall tax implications as well as any legal or operational considerations.

S corporation owners can potentially increase their QBI deduction and optimize their overall tax position by implementing these strategies. It should be noted that these strategies must be implemented in accordance with tax laws and regulations. It is strongly advised to consult with a tax professional or accountant to ensure that the strategies are tailored to the specific circumstances of the business and comply with IRS guidelines.

Keep in mind that the QBI deduction has specific rules and limitations and that each business's situation is unique. As a result, professional advice is required to accurately assess and implement the strategies that will provide the greatest tax benefits while remaining in compliance with tax regulations.

6.5 QBI Deduction Interaction with Other Tax Provisions and Deductions

In this section, we look at how the Qualified Business Income (QBI) deduction interacts with other tax provisions and deductions, giving S corporation owners valuable insights into how to best optimize their overall tax position. Understanding these interactions enables owners to make educated decisions that maximize their tax advantages. The Section 199A deduction, self-employment taxes, and retirement plan contributions are some of the key areas where the QBI deduction interacts with other provisions and deductions.

1. **Section 199A Deduction:** The QBI deduction is a component of the Section 199A deduction, which provides a tax break for certain pass-through businesses. Section 199A allows qualifying taxpayers to deduct up to 20% of their qualified business income. It's worth noting that the QBI deduction is calculated before any other deductions, such as the self-employment tax deduction or retirement plan contributions, are applied. Understanding how the QBI deduction fits into the larger Section 199A deduction can assist S corporation owners in determining the total tax benefits available to them.

2. **Self-Employment Taxes:** The QBI deduction does not directly reduce self-employment taxes. Self-employment taxes include the taxes that both employees and employers typically pay for Social Security and Medicare. The QBI deduction, on the other hand, indirectly reduces self-employment taxes by lowering the taxable income on which these taxes are assessed. S corporation owners can potentially reduce their self-

employment tax liability by reducing taxable income through the QBI deduction and other applicable deductions.

3. **Contributions to Retirement Plans:** S corporation owners frequently contribute to retirement plans, such as SEP-IRAs or individual 401(k) plans, to save for retirement while reaping tax benefits. The QBI deduction has no effect on retirement plan contributions. The QBI deduction, on the other hand, indirectly increases the available funds that owners can allocate to retirement plan contributions by lowering taxable income. When considering the tax-deferred growth and potential deductions associated with retirement plan contributions, this can be especially beneficial.

S corporation owners can make strategic decisions by understanding how the QBI deduction interacts with other tax provisions and deductions. Owners can assess the overall tax benefits of various options, such as maximizing retirement plan contributions while leveraging the QBI deduction, by taking these interactions into account. To fully understand the specific implications and optimize the interactions between the QBI deduction and other tax provisions, it is critical to consult with a tax professional or accountant.

Remember that tax laws and regulations can change at any time and that each taxpayer's situation is unique. As a result, seeking professional advice and staying current on tax regulations are critical for accurately assessing and implementing strategies that maximize available tax benefits.

6.6 Real-Life Scenarios Demonstrating the Impact of the QBI Deduction on Tax Savings

We present real-life scenarios in this section to demonstrate the practical impact of the Qualified Business Income (QBI) deduction on tax savings for S corporation owners. These examples demonstrate how the deduction can significantly reduce taxable income and generate significant tax savings.

Scenario 1: Jane's Consulting Company

Jane owns an S corporation and runs a successful consulting firm. Her qualified business income for the year is $200,000, and she meets all of the QBI deduction requirements. She is in the phase-out range based on her taxable income. Her taxable income would be subject to regular tax rates if she did not take the QBI deduction. She can, however, deduct 20% of her qualified business income using the QBI deduction. Her taxable income is reduced by $40,000 as a result of this deduction, resulting in a lower overall tax liability.

Scenario 2: Mark's Rental Properties

Mark is the owner of an S corporation that earns money from rental properties. His qualified business income for the year is $150,000, and he meets the QBI deduction criteria. Mark, as a landlord, is classified as a specified service trade or business (SSTB), subject to certain restrictions. He is, however, below the taxable income level at which the deduction begins to phase out. Mark can claim a $30,000 QBI deduction, lowering his taxable income and resulting in significant tax savings.

These examples show the direct impact of the QBI deduction on tax savings for S corporation owners. Owners can significantly reduce their taxable income and, as a result, their overall tax liability by taking advantage of the deduction. Individual circumstances, such as the amount of qualified business income, taxable income, and other relevant factors, will determine the specific tax savings.

It should be noted that these are simplified examples for illustrative purposes only. Each taxpayer's situation is unique, and the actual tax savings will depend on a variety of elements, including particular deductions, credits, and tax rates. It is best to consult with a qualified tax professional to accurately assess potential tax savings and determine the most advantageous strategies based on individual circumstances.

Furthermore, because tax laws can change over time, it is critical to stay up to date on any updates or changes to the QBI deduction rules and regulations. Keeping up with these developments allows S corporation owners to make informed decisions and take advantage of the available tax savings provided by the QBI deduction.

6.7 QBI Deduction Rules and Regulations Updates and Changes

It is critical for S corporation owners to stay current on the latest updates and changes to the Qualified Business Income (QBI) deduction rules and regulations. Understanding any recent updates, modifications, or clarifications is critical for accurately determining eligibility and calculating the deduction. This section emphasizes the importance of staying informed and provides examples of recent changes that may have an impact on the QBI deduction.

Example 1: IRS Industry-Specific Guidance

The IRS issues guidance on a regular basis that clarifies various aspects of the QBI deduction. For example, they may issue specific guidance addressing how the deduction applies to unique circumstances within those industries or professions. Keeping up to date on industry-specific guidance ensures that S corporation owners in those industries can accurately assess their eligibility and calculate the deduction.

Example 2: Legislative Amendments or Changes

Legislative changes or amendments to tax laws can have an immediate impact on the QBI deduction. These modifications could include changes to eligibility criteria, calculation methods, phase-out thresholds, or income-based limitations. To ensure compliance with current rules and maximize available deductions, S corporation owners must stay up to date on any legislative changes.

Example 3: Notices and Rulings from the Internal Revenue Service

The IRS issues notices and rulings on a regular basis that provide additional guidance on the QBI deduction. These notices may address specific issues or scenarios not previously addressed by the regulations. Owners of S corporations should pay close attention to these notices and rulings because they can provide valuable insights and clarification on the interpretation and application of the deduction.

S corporation owners can ensure compliance with the latest guidelines and take advantage of any new opportunities by staying informed about updates and changes to the QBI deduction rules and regulations. To stay up to date on any recent updates, it is recommended that you consult with a knowledgeable tax professional or access reputable sources such as the IRS website or tax publications. Keeping up with these changes enables S corporation owners to accurately determine their QBI deduction eligibility and optimize their tax planning strategies accordingly.

6.8 Reporting and Documentation Tips to Support the QBI Deduction

When claiming the Qualified Business Income (QBI) deduction, accurate reporting and thorough documentation are required. This section provides helpful hints and best practices for ensuring accurate reporting and support for the deduction on tax returns. Following these guidelines, S corporation owners can confidently claim the QBI deduction and be well-prepared for an IRS audit.

1. **Maintain Detailed Records:** Keep detailed records of all business income and expenses. Invoices, receipts, bank statements, and financial statements are all examples. It is critical to keep accurate and up-to-date records in order to substantiate the QBI deduction and demonstrate the accuracy of reported income and expenses.

2. **Separate Business and Personal Expenses:** Make a clear distinction between personal and business expenses. This distinction ensures that only qualified business income is eligible for the QBI deduction. Keeping separate bank accounts and credit cards for business and personal use can help to simplify the process.

3. **Record Business Activities:** Keep track of business activities, such as the types of services or products offered, client contracts, and project details. This documentation backs up the classification of income as qualified business income, ensuring its deductibility.

4. **Track Hours Worked:** For S corporation owners who qualify under the "SSTB" limitation, keep accurate time records for each business activity. This information is used to determine whether the business activity falls under a specific service trade or business, which influences eligibility for the QBI deduction.

5. **Consult a Tax Professional:** Seek the advice of a qualified tax professional who is familiar with the QBI deduction. They can offer expert advice tailored to your specific situation and assist you in ensuring accurate reporting and compliance with IRS regulations.

6. **Stay informed:** Review updates and publications from the IRS and other reliable sources on a regular basis to stay up to date on any changes or clarifications to the QBI deduction. Knowing the most recent guidelines and interpretations ensures accurate reporting and reduces the possibility of errors or omissions.

7. **Use Reliable Software or Tools:** Use dependable accounting software or tools designed specifically to track income and expenses and calculate the QBI deduction. These tools can help to speed up the reporting process and reduce the possibility of calculation errors.

8. **Documentation:** Keep all supporting documents, such as financial records, invoices, contracts, and any other relevant documentation, for at least three to seven years. This ensures

that you have the documentation needed to support the QBI deduction if the IRS requests it.

S corporation owners can confidently claim the QBI deduction and have the necessary evidence to substantiate their eligibility and compliance with IRS regulations if they follow these tips for accurate reporting and documentation. Proper documentation not only supports the deduction, but also ensures peace of mind and a smooth tax-filing process.

Conclusion

The Qualified Business Income (QBI) deduction allows S corporation owners to reduce their taxable income and keep a larger portion of their earnings. However, it is critical to understand that the information in this chapter is intended to be general in nature and should not be construed as personalized advice. S corporation owners should seek the advice of a qualified tax professional or accountant to maximize the benefits of the QBI deduction and ensure compliance with the ever-changing tax regulations.

These experts have the expertise and knowledge to provide tailored advice based on individual circumstances, assisting owners in navigating the complexities of the deduction and maximizing their tax savings. S corporation owners can confidently leverage the benefits of the QBI deduction and make informed decisions that align with their financial goals by working with a trusted advisor.

Chapter 7: Mitigating Self-Employment Taxes as an S Corporation

Introduction

The S-corporation structure provides a distinct advantage for small business owners by allowing them to reduce self-employment taxes. This chapter delves into effective strategies and techniques for reducing self-employment tax liabilities while maintaining IRS compliance.

Key topics covered in this chapter include:

1. Understanding self-employment taxes and their impact on small business owners.
2. Comparing self-employment taxes for different business entities, including sole proprietorships and partnerships.
3. Exploring the concept of reasonable compensation and its influence on self-employment taxes.
4. Strategies for optimizing salary and distributions to minimize self-employment tax liability.
5. Utilizing retirement plans and fringe benefits to reduce self-employment taxes.
6. Evaluating the impact of the Tax Cuts and Jobs Act on self-employment taxes.
7. Case studies illustrating effective self-employment tax mitigation techniques.
8. Compliance considerations and best practices for self-employment tax planning.

By implementing strategic measures to mitigate self-employment taxes, S corporation owners can significantly increase their after-tax income and overall financial stability.

7.1 Self-Employment Taxes: What They Mean for Small Business Owners

This section provides a thorough explanation of self-employment taxes, including their calculation and the significant implications for small business owners' income. It emphasizes the importance of effectively managing self-employment taxes to maximize after-tax income by providing a comprehensive overview.

Individuals who work for themselves, such as independent contractors, freelancers, and S corporation owners, must pay self-employment taxes. These taxes are made up of two parts: the Social Security tax and the Medicare tax. The current Social Security tax rate is 12.4% of eligible income, while the Medicare tax rate is 2.9%.

Self-employment taxes can have a significant impact on small business owners. Self-employed individuals are responsible for both the employer and employee portions of Social Security and Medicare taxes, as opposed to employees who have their Social Security and Medicare taxes shared with their employers. As a result, they bear the entire burden of these taxes, resulting in a higher overall tax liability.

It is critical for small business owners to properly manage self-employment taxes in order to maximize their after-tax income. Individuals can accurately estimate their tax liability and plan accordingly if they understand how these taxes are calculated. Furthermore, investigating strategies to reduce self-employment taxes can result in significant tax savings.

Several strategies can be used to reduce the impact of self-employment taxes. Maximizing allowable deductions, such as business expenses and self-employed retirement contributions, for example, can reduce taxable income and, as a result, the overall tax liability. Furthermore, considering the impact of the business structure, such as operating as a S corporation, can provide additional tax planning opportunities.

Effective self-employment tax management necessitates ongoing monitoring and proactive tax planning. Small business owners can take advantage of any available deductions, credits, or exemptions by staying up to date on the latest tax laws and regulations. This enables them to optimize their tax situation and increase their after-tax income.

To summarize, small business owners must understand the calculation and implications of self-employment taxes. Individuals can reduce their tax burden and maximize their after-tax income by effectively managing these taxes. Small business owners can navigate the complexities of self-employment taxes and ensure financial success with proper knowledge and proactive tax planning.

7.2 A Comparison of Self-Employment Taxes for Various Business Entities

This section delves into the differences in self-employment taxes between various business entities, such as sole proprietorships, partnerships, and S corporations. Business owners can make informed decisions about the most tax-efficient structure for their company by understanding the comparative tax implications.

1. Sole Proprietorships

Individuals who operate their businesses as an unincorporated entity are known as sole proprietors. They report their business income and expenses on Schedule C of their personal tax return for tax purposes. Sole proprietors are responsible for both the employer and employee portions of Social Security and Medicare taxes when it comes to self-employment taxes. As a result, they bear the full burden of these taxes, potentially resulting in a higher overall tax liability.

2. Partnerships

Two or more people can form a partnership, which is a business entity that shares ownership and control. Partners in a partnership, like sole proprietors, are subject to self-employment taxes. Each partner is responsible for self-employment taxes on their portion of the partnership's earnings. Partners' self-employment tax is calculated based on their distributive share of partnership income, and they must pay both the employer and employee portions.

3. S Corporations

S-corporations are distinct business entities that provide tax benefits. Unlike sole proprietors and partners, S corporation owners can reduce their self-employment taxes. While S corporation owners receive business income, they are only required to pay self-employment taxes on the portion of their earnings designated as reasonable compensation. This pay should be based on the fair market value of the services they provide to the company. Any additional income received as S corporation distributions is not subject to self-employment taxes.

Business owners who choose S corporation status may be able to reduce their self-employment tax liability. It is important to note, however, that the IRS closely examines the allocation of salary versus distributions to ensure that reasonable compensation is paid. The salary must be reasonable and commensurate with the owner's services.

When comparing self-employment taxes for different business entities, other factors such as liability protection, administrative requirements, and the nature of the business must be considered. While minimizing self-employment taxes is important, it should not be the only factor to consider when deciding on a business structure.

When deciding on the best business entity, it is strongly advised to consult with a qualified tax professional or accountant. They can assess your specific circumstances, analyze potential tax implications, and advise you on the best structure to meet your tax and business objectives.

Finally, understanding the differences in self-employment taxes among various business entities enables business owners to make informed decisions about the structure of their company. Sole proprietors and partners must pay self-employment taxes on all of their income, whereas S corporation owners can reduce self-employment taxes by allocating reasonable compensation. When deciding on the most tax-efficient structure for your company, it is critical to balance tax considerations with other business factors.

7.3 Exploring the Concept of Reasonable Compensation

This section delves into the concept of reasonable compensation and its implications for S corporation owners when it comes to self-employment taxes. We explain the IRS guidelines for determining a reasonable salary and emphasize the importance of aligning compensation with industry standards to avoid IRS scrutiny.

As the owner of an S corporation, you must distinguish between two types of income: salary and distributions. While self-employment taxes apply to salaries, distributions do not. The IRS requires S corporation owners to be paid a fair wage for the services they provide to the company. This requirement exists to prevent owners from avoiding self-employment taxes by classifying all income as distributions.

The nature of the work performed, the industry in which the business operates, the owner's qualifications and experience, and the overall profitability of the company are all considered when determining reasonable compensation. Because reasonable compensation varies depending on individual circumstances, the IRS does not provide specific guidelines for calculating it. However, it is critical to ensure that the owner's salary is reasonable and comparable to that of a non-owner employee performing similar duties.

S corporation owners can demonstrate that they are following fair and customary practices by aligning compensation with industry standards. It aids in defending against potential IRS challenges and scrutiny. If an owner's salary is disproportionately low in comparison to industry benchmarks, the IRS may reclassify distributions as salary, subjecting them to self-employment taxes and potentially levying penalties and interest.

Business owners can use industry salary surveys, consult with human resources professionals or industry experts, or analyze compensation data from comparable positions in similar businesses to determine a reasonable salary. These resources can provide useful information about the appropriate salary range for the owner's role and responsibilities.

It should be noted that determining reasonable compensation is a subjective matter that can be open to interpretation. As a result, it's a good idea to keep track of the factors that went into determining the salary, such as job descriptions, industry research, and expert opinions. Maintaining accurate records and documentation shows a good-faith effort to comply with IRS guidelines and can help substantiate the reasonableness of the compensation if it is challenged.

Finally, S corporation owners must understand the concept of reasonable compensation in order to effectively manage self-employment taxes. Owners can reduce the risk of IRS scrutiny and ensure compliance with tax regulations by aligning compensation with industry standards and documenting the factors considered.

Consulting with a qualified tax professional or accountant can help you determine a reasonable salary that balances tax considerations with industry norms.

7.4 Salary and Distribution Optimization Strategies

In this section, we look at strategies for optimizing salary and distributions for S corporation owners in order to reduce self-employment tax liability. Owners can implement an optimal strategy that reduces their tax burden while remaining compliant with IRS regulations by striking the right balance between reasonable compensation and profit distributions.

1. **Determine a Reasonable Salary:** As previously discussed, it is critical to establish a reasonable salary that is in line with industry standards and reflects the services provided by the owner. Owners can strike a balance that minimizes self-employment taxes while avoiding IRS scrutiny by ensuring that the salary is neither excessively low nor excessively high.

2. **Consider Tax Savings with Distributions:** Distributions to S corporation owners are not subject to self-employment taxes, unlike salary. Owners can reduce their self-employment tax liability by distributing profits as dividends or shareholder distributions rather than salary. However, in order to comply with IRS guidelines, a reasonable salary component must be maintained.

3. **Assess the Impact of the Qualified Business Income Deduction:** As discussed in Chapter 6, the Qualified Business Income (QBI) deduction can provide significant tax benefits to

S corporation owners. Owners can reduce their taxable income and, as a result, their self-employment tax liability by maximizing the QBI deduction through strategies such as optimizing salary levels and utilizing allowable deductions.

4. **Seek Professional Advice:** When optimizing salary and distributions, it is critical to consult with a qualified tax professional or accountant who is familiar with S corporation taxation. These professionals can examine the company's specific circumstances, industry benchmarks, and IRS regulations to create a tailored strategy that reduces self-employment tax liability while ensuring compliance.

5. **Review and Adjust Compensation on a Regular Basis:** It is critical to review and adjust compensation on a regular basis to ensure that it remains aligned with changing business circumstances, industry norms, and IRS guidelines. Adjustments may be required to optimize the salary and distribution strategy for maximum tax efficiency as the business grows, profitability fluctuates, or industry standards evolve.

While optimizing salary and distributions can reduce self-employment tax liability, owners must also ensure compliance with IRS guidelines and keep documentation to support the reasonableness of compensation. Each company's situation is unique, and expert advice tailored to specific circumstances is strongly advised.

S corporation owners can optimize their salary and distribution structure by implementing these strategic approaches, striking a balance that minimizes self-employment tax liability while remaining compliant with IRS regulations. Maximizing tax savings through careful planning and professional guidance can significantly boost a company's after-tax profitability.

7.5 Utilizing Retirement Plans and Fringe Benefits

We will look at how S corporation owners can use retirement plans and fringe benefits to effectively reduce self-employment taxes in this section. Owners can reduce their taxable income and increase their overall tax savings by strategically implementing retirement plans and providing fringe benefits to employees.

1. **Retirement Plans**

    Retirement plans, such as 401(k) plans, SEP IRAs (Simplified Employee Pension Individual Retirement Accounts), and SIMPLE IRAs (Savings Incentive Match Plan for Employees Individual Retirement Accounts), provide tax benefits to both owners and employees. Contributing to these plans allows owners to reduce their taxable income, lowering their self-employment tax liability. Contributions made by the owner are generally tax deductible and grow tax-deferred until retirement.

2. **Employee Fringe Benefits**

    Offering fringe benefits to employees can also help S corporation owners reduce self-employment taxes. Health insurance, life insurance, disability insurance, dependent care assistance, and transportation benefits are examples of fringe benefits. These benefits are typically deductible as business expenses, lowering the owner's taxable income and, thus, self-employment tax liability.

3. Seek Professional Advice

Implementing retirement plans and fringe benefits necessitates careful thought and adherence to IRS rules and regulations. It is critical to consult with a qualified financial advisor or employee benefits specialist to ensure proper plan design, eligibility requirements, contribution limits, and compliance with applicable tax laws. Based on the unique circumstances and goals of the business, these professionals can assist owners in selecting the best retirement plan and fringe benefit options.

4. Consider the Impact on Employees

When implementing retirement plans and fringe benefits, business owners should consider the impact on employees. These perks can help to attract and retain talented employees, increase employee morale and job satisfaction, and contribute to a positive work environment. S corporation owners can create a win-win situation for both the business and its employees by offering competitive retirement plans and valuable fringe benefits.

To comply with IRS regulations, retirement plans and fringe benefits must be properly established and administered. To ensure ongoing compliance and alignment with changing business needs, regular reviews and updates should be performed.

S corporation owners can effectively reduce their taxable income, lower their self-employment tax liability, and create a more attractive and competitive work environment for their employees by strategically utilizing retirement plans and providing valuable fringe benefits. Seeking professional advice and following IRS guidelines are required for successful implementation and compliance with applicable tax laws.

7.6 Assessing the Tax Cuts and Jobs Act's Impact

In this section, we will look at the specific provisions of the Tax Cuts and Jobs Act (TCJA) that affect self-employment taxes. To effectively plan their self-employment tax mitigation strategies, business owners must understand any changes or updates to the tax code as a result of the TCJA.

1. **Qualified Business Income Deduction:**

   The TCJA introduced the Qualified Business Income (QBI) deduction, which enables eligible businesses, including S corporations, to deduct up to 20% of their qualified business income. For eligible S corporation owners, this deduction can significantly reduce taxable income and, as a result, self-employment tax liability. Understanding the complexities of the QBI deduction and how it interacts with self-employment taxes is critical for getting the most out of your tax refund.

2. **Changes in Tax Rates and Brackets:**

   The TCJA altered individual tax rates and brackets. It is critical to consider how these changes will affect self-employment taxes for S corporation owners. Owners can adjust their salary and distribution strategies to optimize their overall tax position and minimize self-employment tax liability by taking the new tax rates and brackets into account.

3. **State and Local Tax Deduction Limitations:**
   The TCJA imposed limits on the deduction for state and local taxes (SALT). This restriction may have an impact on self-employment taxes, particularly for owners who live in states with high income tax rates. Understanding the impact of the SALT deduction limitation and considering alternative strategies for managing state and local taxes are critical.

4. **Additional Considerations:**
   While the TCJA primarily focused on individual and corporate tax reforms, S corporation owners should thoroughly review the legislation to identify any provisions or changes that may have an indirect impact on self-employment taxes. This could include changes to depreciation rules, changes to business expense deductions, or changes to other tax provisions that affect S corporation owners' overall tax liability.

Staying informed about the specific provisions of the TCJA that affect self-employment taxes allows S corporation owners to adjust their strategies and capitalize on any new tax savings opportunities. It is recommended that you consult with a qualified tax professional or accountant to fully understand the TCJA's implications and ensure compliance with the most recent tax regulations.

It is important to remember that tax laws change over time and that periodic updates and reviews of tax planning strategies are required to stay in compliance and maximize tax benefits.

7.7 Case Studies Illustrating Effective Self-Employment Tax Mitigation Techniques

In this section, we present real-life case studies that illustrate successful self-employment tax mitigation techniques. These examples provide practical insights into how business owners can implement the strategies discussed throughout the chapter to achieve substantial tax savings. By examining these case studies, readers can gain a better understanding of how to apply these techniques in their own situations.

Case Study 1: Optimal Salary-Distribution Balance

John is the owner of an S corporation in the technology industry. After consulting with a tax professional, he realizes the importance of balancing his salary and distributions to minimize self-employment taxes. By analyzing his business's financials and considering industry benchmarks, John determines a reasonable salary that aligns with his role and responsibilities. He then strategically distributes the remaining profits as dividends, which are not subject to self-employment taxes. Through this approach, John effectively reduces his self-employment tax liability while remaining compliant with IRS guidelines.

Case Study 2: Retirement Plan Maximization

Sarah owns an S corporation in the healthcare sector. To mitigate self-employment taxes, she explores the use of retirement plans. After consulting with a financial advisor, Sarah establishes a solo 401(k) plan, allowing her to contribute a significant portion of her income to the retirement account. By contributing to the plan, Sarah reduces her taxable income and, consequently, her self-employment tax liability. Additionally, she benefits from tax-deferred growth and the opportunity to save for retirement.

Case Study 3: Fringe Benefits Optimization

Michael operates an S corporation in the consulting industry. He seeks ways to reduce his self-employment taxes while providing additional benefits to his employees. By implementing a comprehensive fringe benefits package, including health insurance, life insurance, and flexible spending accounts, Michael takes advantage of the tax deductions associated with these benefits. The deductions lower his taxable income and, subsequently, his self-employment tax liability. Moreover, the attractive benefits package helps attract and retain top talent in his industry.

These case studies demonstrate that strategic planning and implementation of self-employment tax mitigation techniques can yield significant tax savings for S corporation owners. However, it is essential to remember that each business's circumstances are unique, and consulting with a qualified tax professional is crucial to tailoring these strategies to specific situations.

By studying these real-life examples and considering the lessons learned, readers can gain valuable insights into the practical application of self-employment tax mitigation techniques. Implementing similar strategies, customized to their own business needs, can help S-corporation owners achieve substantial tax savings and increase their after-tax income.

7.8 Compliance Issues and Best Practices

This section discusses compliance issues and best practices for self-employment tax planning. To ensure compliance and avoid potential penalties, it is critical to follow IRS regulations and keep accurate records. By adhering to these best practices, business owners can successfully navigate the complexities of self-employment taxes while remaining on the right side of the law.

1. **Accurate Record-Keeping:** It is critical for self-employment tax compliance to keep detailed and organized records. Keep track of your income, expenses, payroll records, and any other pertinent financial data. Accurate records will aid in the support of deductions, the determination of reasonable compensation, and the demonstration of compliance with IRS guidelines.

2. **Proper Documentation:** Documentation is essential when it comes to self-employment tax planning. Maintain copies of all tax returns, employment contracts, business agreements, and other documents that support your tax positions. This documentation serves as evidence in the event of an IRS audit or investigation.

3. **Speak with a Tax Professional:** Self-employment taxes can be complicated, and regulations are subject to change. It is best to consult with a qualified tax professional or an accountant who specializes in small business taxation. They can provide personalized advice, assist in the optimization of tax strategies, and ensure compliance with the most recent regulations.

4. **Keep up to date:** Tax laws and regulations are subject to change. Keep up with any updates or changes to self-employment tax rules. Subscribe to reputable tax information sources, attend seminars or workshops, and participate in professional networks to stay up-to-date on any changes that may affect your self-employment tax planning.

5. **Filing and Payment Deadlines:** Follow all deadlines for filing tax returns and making tax payments. Penalties and interest charges may be imposed for late filings or payments. Set up reminders and a system to ensure that tax obligations are met on time.

6. **Monitor Changing Circumstances:** Changes in your business structure, income levels, and any other relevant factors that may impact your self-employment tax planning should be closely monitored. Adapt your strategies to maximize tax savings while remaining in compliance with IRS regulations.

7. **Seek Professional Advice in Complex Situations:** If you encounter complex situations or have unusual circumstances, such as cross-border activities or industry-specific tax considerations, consult with a tax professional who specializes in those areas. Their knowledge can assist you in navigating the complexities and ensuring accurate and compliant tax planning.

Business owners can reduce the risk of errors, penalties, and audits by following these compliance considerations and best practices.

They can confidently navigate the world of self-employment taxes, maximizing tax benefits while staying within the legal parameters. Remember that getting professional advice and keeping accurate records are critical components of effective self-employment tax planning.

Conclusion

Finally, by implementing strategic measures to reduce self-employment taxes, S corporation owners can significantly increase their after-tax income and overall financial stability. The information in this chapter is a good starting point, but business owners should consult with a qualified tax professional or accountant to get personalized advice based on their specific circumstances.

Because every business situation is unique, navigating the complexities of self-employment taxes requires expert guidance. A qualified tax professional can develop strategies that are tailored to your specific needs and goals. They can assist you in optimizing your tax position, minimizing self-employment tax liability, and ensuring IRS compliance.

Remember that the self-employment tax landscape is subject to change, and staying up-to-date on updates and changes to tax laws is critical. You can stay ahead of any changes that may affect your self-employment tax planning by collaborating with a knowledgeable tax professional.

Finally, S corporation owners can achieve significant tax savings, increase their after-tax income, and maintain financial stability by implementing effective self-employment tax mitigation strategies and working alongside a trusted tax professional. Take proactive measures, seek expert advice, and position yourself for success as you navigate the complicated world of self-employment taxes.

Chapter 8: Advanced Tax Planning Strategies for S Corporation Owners

Introduction

Understanding advanced tax planning strategies becomes critical as S corporation owners navigate the complex world of taxation. This chapter delves into sophisticated techniques and tactics for S corporation owners to maximize tax savings, deductions, and overall financial efficiency.

Key topics covered in this chapter include:

1. Overview of advanced tax planning and its benefits for S corporation owners.
2. Leveraging tax brackets and income shifting strategies to minimize overall tax liability.
3. Utilizing tax credits and incentives specific to S corporations to reduce tax obligations.
4. Exploring tax deferral strategies, such as like-kind exchanges and installment sales.
5. Implementing tax-efficient compensation structures for owners and key employees.
6. Harnessing the power of fringe benefits and employee perks to minimize taxable income.
7. Evaluating the role of trusts and estate planning in S corporation taxation.
8. Case studies showcasing the application of advanced tax planning strategies.

S corporation owners can optimize their tax position, maximize savings, and achieve long-term financial success by incorporating advanced tax planning strategies into their financial management. It is critical to seek personalized advice from a qualified tax professional or accountant based on individual circumstances. S corporation owners can navigate the complexities of advanced tax planning with expert guidance and realize the full potential of their tax strategy.

8.1 A summary of advanced tax planning and its advantages for S corporation owners

In this section, we provide a comprehensive overview of advanced tax planning and its specific benefits for S corporation owners. We look at strategic tax planning, which goes beyond basic compliance and empowers business owners to manage their tax liabilities and maximize their financial outcomes.

Advanced tax planning entails a proactive and comprehensive approach to taxation, taking into account a wide range of factors such as income sources, deductions, credits, and long-term financial goals. S corporation owners can optimize their tax position and achieve significant benefits by utilizing sophisticated strategies and techniques.

The advantages of advance tax planning for S corporation owners are numerous. For starters, it allows for the reduction of tax liabilities by strategically utilizing S corporation-specific deductions, credits, and incentives. Owners can maximize tax savings and increase after-tax income by delving into the complexities of the tax code and tailoring strategies to their specific circumstances.

Second, advanced tax planning allows owners to effectively navigate the complexities of tax brackets and income shifting strategies. S corporation owners can take advantage of lower tax rates and minimize their overall tax liability by strategically allocating income among family members or entities.

In addition, advanced tax planning allows for tax deferral strategies such as like-kind exchanges and installment sales. These strategies enable owners to postpone the recognition of taxable income, giving them more flexibility and the potential for tax savings in the short and long term.

Also, S corporation owners can reduce tax liabilities while attracting and retaining valuable talent within their organizations by implementing tax-efficient compensation structures for owners and key employees.

Furthermore, using fringe benefits and employee perks within the limits of tax regulations can help reduce taxable income for both the business and its employees. This not only improves the organization's overall financial efficiency, but it also contributes to employee satisfaction and retention.

Finally, advanced tax planning recognizes the significance of trusts and estate planning in the taxation of S corporations. Owners can ensure tax-efficient wealth transfer and succession planning by incorporating proper estate planning strategies, preserving the integrity of the S corporation structure, and maximizing long-term financial success.

S corporation owners can gain a competitive advantage in managing their tax liabilities and maximizing their financial outcomes by implementing advanced tax planning strategies. Working with a qualified tax professional or accountant who can provide personalized advice based on individual circumstances and guide owners through the complexities of advanced tax planning is essential. S corporation owners can optimize their tax position, maximize savings, and achieve their long-term financial goals with expert guidance and proactive tax planning.

8.2 Taking advantage of tax brackets and income shifting strategies

This section looks at how to use tax brackets and income shifting strategies to reduce overall tax liability for S corporation owners. Owners can take advantage of lower tax rates and optimize their tax position by strategically distributing income among family members or entities.

Tax brackets represent the various income levels that are taxed at different rates. S corporation owners can strategically manage their income to minimize the amount of taxable income that falls into higher tax brackets by understanding the progressive nature of tax brackets.

The distribution of income to family members in lower tax brackets is a common income-shifting strategy. You can accomplish this by paying family members for their services. By doing so, the S corporation's overall tax liability can be reduced because the income is taxed at the lower rates applicable to those family members.

Income shifting strategies must be implemented in accordance with IRS regulations and should reflect the fair market value of services rendered. The IRS investigates income shifting arrangements to ensure they are not solely used for tax avoidance. As a result, seeking professional advice and ensuring that these strategies are properly structured and documented are critical.

S corporation owners can consider income shifting strategies such as partnerships or limited liability companies (LLCs) in addition to income shifting among family members. Owners can effectively manage their tax liability by taking advantage of the tax rates applicable to each entity, appropriately structuring business relationships, and allocating income among different entities.

While income shifting strategies can provide tax benefits, they must be implemented within the confines of tax laws and regulations. Working with a qualified tax professional or accountant to ensure compliance and navigate the complexities of these strategies is essential.

S corporation owners can optimize their tax position by minimizing the amount of income subject to higher tax rates by leveraging tax brackets and implementing income shifting strategies. However, working with professionals who can provide advice tailored to individual circumstances and ensure compliance with applicable tax laws and regulations is essential.

8.3 Taking advantage of S corporation-specific tax breaks and incentives

In this section, we will look at the tax credits and incentives available to S corporations. S-corporation owners can significantly reduce their tax obligations and increase their after-tax income by understanding and leveraging these incentives.

Tax credits are valuable tools that directly reduce a company's tax liability. S corporations may be eligible for tax breaks such as the R&D Tax Credit, the Work Opportunity Tax Credit (WOTC), and the Small Business Health Care Tax Credit. These credits allow S corporations to reduce their tax liability by offsetting some of their qualifying expenses or providing incentives for specific activities.

For example, the R&D Tax Credit encourages businesses to invest in research and development. S corporations that engage in qualified research activities may claim a credit for eligible expenses such as wages, supplies, and contract research. S corporation owners can reduce their tax liability and allocate more resources to innovation and growth by taking advantage of this credit.

The WOTC is another valuable credit that encourages employers to hire certain targeted groups, such as veterans, long-term unemployed individuals, and government assistance recipients. S corporations that hire people from these targeted groups can claim a tax credit based on a percentage of the employee's wages, allowing them to reduce their tax liability while also supporting workforce diversity and inclusion.

Furthermore, S corporations that offer health insurance to their employees may be eligible for the Small Business Health Care Tax Credit. This credit is intended to help small businesses provide affordable healthcare for their employees. S corporations can claim a credit that offsets a portion of their premium expenses by meeting certain requirements and offering qualified health insurance plans, lowering their overall tax liability.

S corporation owners should be aware of the specific tax credits and incentives available to them, as well as the requirements and limitations associated with each credit. Owners can maximize their benefits by working with a qualified tax professional or accountant to determine which credits they may qualify for.

Owners can effectively reduce their tax obligations and increase their after-tax income by utilizing S corporation-specific tax credits and incentives. However, it is critical to consult with professionals who can provide tailored advice and ensure compliance with applicable tax laws and regulations.

8.4 Exploring tax deferral strategies

In this section, we will look at tax deferral strategies that S corporation owners can use, such as like-kind exchanges and installment sales. These strategies allow you to postpone the recognition of taxable income, giving you more flexibility as well as potential tax savings.

A like-kind exchange, also known as a 1031 exchange, allows S corporation owners to postpone the recognition of capital gains tax on certain property exchanges for similar property. Owners can defer the tax liability that would normally result from a capital gain by reinvesting the proceeds from the sale of property in a similar or "like-kind" property. This strategy has the benefit of preserving capital while allowing it to grow tax-free over time.

The use of installment sales is another tax deferral strategy. S corporation owners can spread the recognition of income over multiple tax years with an installment sale by receiving payments from the buyer in installments rather than a lump sum. Owners can potentially reduce their overall tax burden by deferring the receipt of the full sale proceeds. This strategy is especially useful when selling appreciated assets like real estate or business assets.

While tax deferral strategies can provide significant benefits, they require careful planning and adherence to specific IRS rules and regulations. Like-kind exchanges, for example, have strict timeframes for completion and specific requirements for the types of properties that qualify. Similarly, installment sales must meet certain requirements in order to qualify for tax deferral.

To ensure proper implementation and compliance, S corporation owners should work closely with tax professionals or advisors who specialize in these strategies. They can assist in determining the feasibility and suitability of these deferral strategies based on individual circumstances, as well as provide guidance on meeting the requirements and maximizing the potential tax savings.

S corporation owners can effectively manage their tax liabilities, gain flexibility in their financial planning, and potentially reduce their overall tax burden by utilizing tax deferral strategies such as like-kind exchanges and installment sales. However, professional advice is required to navigate the complexities of these strategies and ensure compliance with applicable tax laws and regulations.

8.5 Putting in place tax-efficient compensation structures

In this section, we will discuss the significance of implementing tax-efficient compensation structures for S corporation owners and key employees. S corporation owners can reduce tax liabilities while remaining in compliance with IRS regulations by strategically structuring compensation packages.

Finding the right balance between salary and distributions is an important aspect of tax-efficient compensation. S corporation owners have the option of receiving both a reasonable salary and profit distributions. Owners can ensure compliance with IRS guidelines and avoid potential scrutiny by setting a reasonable salary that aligns with industry standards and reflects the owner's role and responsibilities.

The benefit of structuring compensation through distributions is that they are exempt from self-employment taxes like Social Security and Medicare. S corporation owners can save significantly on taxes because they only pay self-employment taxes on their salary portion, while distributions are generally taxed at a lower rate.

To avoid potential IRS challenges, it is critical to maintain a reasonable salary level. The IRS scrutinizes compensation structures to ensure that owners are not underreporting their earnings in order to avoid paying self-employment taxes. To determine a reasonable salary based on industry benchmarks and the specific circumstances of the business, it is recommended that you consult with a qualified tax professional or advisor.

S corporation owners can explore other tax-efficient compensation options in addition to salary and distributions. This could include providing employee perks and fringe benefits such as health insurance, retirement plans, educational assistance, or transportation benefits. These benefits may be tax-deductible for the company and may result in tax savings for both the owners and the employees.

It is critical to consider the overall tax implications, compliance with IRS regulations, and the specific needs and goals of the business and its employees when implementing tax-efficient compensation structures. Professional tax advice can assist business owners in designing compensation packages that align with their tax planning goals while remaining in compliance with applicable laws and regulations.

S corporation owners can optimize their tax position, reduce tax liabilities, and improve overall financial efficiency by implementing tax-efficient compensation structures. These strategies not only save money on taxes, but they also help to attract and retain key employees by providing competitive compensation packages.

8.6 Harnessing the Power of Employee Perks and Fringe Benefits

In this section, we will look at how to use fringe benefits and employee perks to reduce taxable income for S corporation owners. S corporation owners can maximize tax savings for both the business and its employees by providing a variety of tax-advantaged benefits.

Non-wage compensation provided to employees in addition to their regular salary or wages is referred to as fringe benefits. These benefits may include everything from health insurance and retirement plans to educational assistance and transportation. S corporation owners can provide additional value to their employees while also taking advantage of tax savings opportunities by providing fringe benefits.

One significant advantage of fringe benefits is that they are frequently tax deductible for the company, lowering taxable income. S corporation owners can provide valuable employee benefits while also enjoying tax benefits by providing benefits such as health insurance, dental and vision plans, life insurance, and disability coverage.

Another effective tool for reducing taxable income is a retirement plan. S corporation owners can set up retirement plans such as 401(k)s, SEP IRAs, or Savings Incentive Match Plan for Employees (SIMPLE) IRAs. These plans not only assist employees in saving for retirement, but they also provide tax benefits. Contributions made by the company to these retirement plans are tax deductible, lowering the company's taxable income.

Education assistance programs can be beneficial to both employees and businesses. Employees can receive educational assistance from S corporation owners, such as tuition reimbursement for job-related courses or educational scholarships. Up to a certain limit, the company can deduct these costs from the employees' taxable income.

Tax advantages can be obtained from transportation benefits such as commuter benefits or parking subsidies. Owners of S corporations can provide qualified transportation fringe benefits, which allow employees to pay for commuting expenses with pre-tax dollars. This reduces employees' taxable income and provides tax savings for both the company and its employees.

When implementing fringe benefits and employee perks, it is critical to follow IRS regulations and ensure that the benefits provided are tax-deductible. To navigate the complexities of fringe benefit programs and ensure compliance with tax laws, it is recommended that you consult with a qualified tax professional or benefits specialist.

S-corporation owners can reduce taxable income for both the business and its employees by leveraging the power of fringe benefits and employee perks. These strategies not only save taxes, but they also improve employee satisfaction and retention. Offering valuable benefits can help attract and retain top talent while also optimizing the company's overall tax position.

8.7 Trusts and Estate Planning: What Role Do They Play?

In this section, we will examine the role of trusts and estate planning in S corporation taxation. We will go over how proper estate planning can help with tax-efficient wealth transfer and succession planning while maintaining the S corporation structure's integrity.

Trusts can be very useful in estate planning for S corporation owners. Owners can transfer assets and ownership interests to beneficiaries while maintaining control and minimizing tax implications by establishing trusts. The revocable living trust is a common trust used in estate planning because it allows owners to retain control over their assets during their lifetime while ensuring a seamless transfer of assets to designated beneficiaries upon their death.

S corporation owners can achieve tax efficiency by utilizing various estate planning techniques through trusts. For example, using grantor retained annuity trusts (GRATs) or intentionally defective grantor trusts (IDGTs) to leverage valuation discounts or freeze the value of transferred assets for tax purposes can help minimize estate and gift taxes. When transferring S corporation shares to future generations or family members, these strategies can be especially beneficial.

Succession planning is an important aspect of estate planning for S corporation owners. Owners can ensure the smooth continuation of the business while minimizing tax consequences by developing a well-defined plan for the transition of ownership and management. This could include drafting a buy-sell agreement, forming a family limited partnership (FLP), or employing other business succession planning tools that align with the owner's goals and objectives.

While trusts and estate planning can provide significant tax benefits and facilitate wealth transfer, it is critical to consider the potential impact on the S corporation structure and its eligibility for certain tax benefits. Certain restrictions and limitations, such as the rules governing the number and types of shareholders in an S corporation, may apply.

It is best to seek the advice of an experienced estate planning attorney or tax professional when navigating the complexities of trusts and estate planning for S corporation taxation. These professionals can provide personalized advice based on the S corporation owner's specific circumstances and goals, ensuring compliance with tax laws and maximizing tax efficiency in wealth transfer and succession planning.

Owners can proactively plan for the future, preserve their wealth, and establish a solid foundation for the continued success of their business by properly evaluating the role of trusts and estate planning in S corporation taxation.

8.8 Case studies demonstrating sophisticated tax planning strategies

In this section, we will present real-world case studies that demonstrate the use of advanced tax planning strategies. These examples will show how S corporation owners can use sophisticated techniques to maximize tax savings and achieve favorable financial results.

Case Study 1: Income Diversification Strategy

Jane is the owner of an S corporation that generates a lot of money. She wants to reduce her overall tax liability by taking advantage of tax brackets and income shifting strategies. Jane decides to use an income shifting strategy by hiring her spouse as an employee of the S corporation after consulting with her tax advisor. She is able to shift a portion of her income to her spouse, who is in a lower tax bracket, by doing so. As a result, the company's overall tax liability is reduced, resulting in significant tax savings for Jane and her family.

Case Study 2: Tax Credits and Incentives

Devin owns an S corporation, which is eligible for certain tax breaks and incentives. He takes advantage of the R&D tax credit by investing in research activities to create new products and improve existing ones. Devin is able to significantly reduce his tax obligations by properly documenting and claiming the R&D tax credit. The tax credit not only reduces his current tax liability, but it also strengthens his company's financial position, allowing for additional investment in innovation and growth.

Case Study 3: Deferred Tax Exchanges

Sarah owns an S corporation and intends to sell a commercial property whose value has increased. Sarah decides to use a tax-deferred exchange, also known as a 1031 exchange, rather than recognize the entire capital gain as taxable income in the year of the sale. Sarah can defer the recognition of the capital gain by reinvesting the sale proceeds in a like-kind property, preserving her cash flow and potentially deferring the tax liability to a later date.

These case studies demonstrate how advanced tax planning strategies for S corporation owners can be put into practice. They demonstrate the potential tax savings and financial benefits of implementing these strategies. However, because every situation is different, the efficacy of these strategies will depend on the particulars of each case as well as on adherence to any applicable tax laws and regulations.

S corporation owners should consult with a qualified tax professional or accountant to analyze their specific situation and develop a tailored tax plan. S corporation owners can navigate the complexities of advanced tax planning and maximize their tax savings while remaining compliant with IRS regulations by leveraging the expertise of professionals and learning from successful case studies.

Conclusion

S corporation owners can optimize their tax position, maximize savings, and set themselves up for long-term financial success by incorporating advanced tax planning strategies into their financial management. However, it is critical to understand that the information in this chapter is intended to be a general guide.

S-corporation owners should consult with a qualified tax professional or accountant to develop a tax plan tailored to their specific circumstances. These professionals can offer personalized advice and guidance, taking into account the unique aspects of the business as well as the ever-changing tax landscape.

S corporation owners can navigate the complexities of advanced tax planning with the assistance of these professionals, making informed decisions and realizing the full potential of their tax strategy. They can achieve their financial objectives while also complying with applicable tax laws and regulations.

Chapter 9: S Corporation Distributions: Dividends, Loans, and Tax Consequences

Introduction

S corporation distributions are critical to providing owners with access to their business profits. Understanding the various types of distributions and their tax implications, on the other hand, is critical for both compliance and informed financial decision-making. This chapter delves into the complexities of S corporation distributions, such as dividends, loans, and the tax implications.

Key topics covered in this chapter include:

1. In the context of S corporation distributions, distinguishing between dividends and loans.

2. The taxation of qualified and non-qualified dividends for S corporation shareholders.

3. Considering the effect of accumulated earnings and the personal holding company tax on distributions.

4. Recognize the tax implications of shareholder loans and their repayment.

5. Techniques for structuring tax-advantaged distributions and debt arrangements.

6. Distribution considerations during the liquidation or sale of a business.

7. S corporation distributions must comply with IRS regulations and reporting requirements.

8. Real-world examples demonstrating the tax implications of various distribution scenarios.

Owners can make informed decisions, maximize tax efficiency, and ensure compliance with tax laws by understanding the nuances of S corporation distributions. This chapter provides valuable insights and guidance to help S corporation owners navigate the complexities of distributions, minimize tax liabilities, and manage their financial affairs effectively.

9.1 Differentiating between dividends and loans in the context of S corporation distributions

In the context of S corporation distributions, distinguishing between dividends and loans is critical. Understanding the distinction between these two types of distributions is critical for both tax and legal purposes.

Dividends: Dividends are a distribution of profits to S corporation shareholders. They are typically paid from the corporation's accumulated earnings and profits and are considered taxable income to the shareholders. Dividends are taxed differently and can be qualified or non-qualified depending on certain criteria. It is critical to correctly identify and report dividends in order to comply with tax laws.

Loans: Loans, on the other hand, involve providing funds to shareholders with the expectation that they will be repaid within a specified timeframe, plus any applicable interest. Loans, unlike dividends, are not taxable income for shareholders at the time they are received. Interest payments on the loans, on the other hand, may be taxed. To ensure that the transaction is treated as a legitimate loan rather than a disguised dividend, it is critical to establish a formal loan agreement and follow all legal and regulatory requirements.

It is critical to distinguish between dividends and loans in order to correctly classify the nature of S corporation distributions. S corporation owners can comply with tax regulations, properly report income, and make informed decisions about their businesses' financial management by correctly identifying whether a distribution is a dividend or a loan.

9.2 The tax treatment of qualified and non-qualified dividends for S corporation owners

Understanding the tax treatment of qualified and non-qualified dividends is critical for S corporation owners in determining the tax implications of their distributions.

Qualified Dividends: Qualified dividends are a type of dividend that meets the Internal Revenue Service's (IRS) criteria. These dividends are subject to a lower tax rate, which is typically lower than the rate on ordinary income. For the dividend to qualify for this preferential tax treatment, a U.S. corporation or a qualified foreign corporation must pay it, and the shareholder must adhere to specific holding period requirements. Form 1099-DIV is used to report qualified dividends, which are taxed at the applicable capital gains tax rate.

Non-Qualified Dividends: Non-qualified dividends are dividends that do not meet the qualifications for qualified dividend status. These dividends are generally taxed at the same rate as ordinary income. Distributions from real estate investment trusts (REITs), certain foreign corporations, and dividends received on employee stock options are examples of non-qualified dividends. Non-qualified dividends, like qualified dividends, are reported on Form 1099-DIV but are taxed at the shareholder's ordinary income tax rate.

For accurate tax reporting, S corporation owners must properly identify and classify dividends as qualified or non-qualified. Owners can effectively plan for their tax obligations, optimize their tax position, and comply with IRS regulations if they understand the tax treatment of these dividends. A qualified tax professional or accountant can provide additional guidance on the specific tax treatment of dividends in individual circumstances.

9.3 Calculating the effect of accumulated earnings and personal holding company tax on distributions

When considering S corporation distributions, consider the impact of accumulated earnings as well as the personal holding company tax. These factors can have an impact on the tax implications of distributions for both the corporation and its shareholders.

Accumulated Earnings: Accumulated earnings are the S corporation's retained profits that have not been distributed to shareholders as dividends. The IRS closely monitors corporations with significant accumulated earnings because it may indicate an attempt to avoid income taxes by retaining earnings rather than distributing them as dividends. If the IRS determines that the accumulated earnings are excessive, it may levy an accumulated earnings tax, which is an additional tax on the retained earnings. To avoid potential tax consequences, S corporation owners must carefully manage and justify the level of accumulated earnings.

Personal Holding Company Tax: The personal holding company tax is a tax imposed on certain closely held corporations that derive a significant portion of their income from passive activities such as dividends, interest, royalties, and rents. This additional tax may apply if an S corporation meets the criteria for a personal holding company. It should be noted that the majority of S corporations do not meet the requirements for personal holding company status. However, if the activities of a S corporation change or it holds passive investments, the personal holding company tax should be assessed to determine its potential impact on distributions.

When considering distributions, S corporation owners must understand the implications of accumulated earnings and the personal holding company tax. Proper management of accumulated earnings and compliance with tax regulations can help reduce tax liabilities and ensure proper distribution treatment. To effectively navigate these complex tax considerations, seek advice from a qualified tax professional or accountant.

9.4 Recognizing the tax implications of shareholder loans and their repayment

It is critical to understand the tax consequences of shareholder loans and their repayment in the context of S corporation distributions. Shareholder loans are funds borrowed from the S corporation's shareholders in the form of loans or advances.

Shareholder Loans: From a tax perspective, shareholder loans are typically considered debt obligations that the S corporation must pay back. When the corporation receives the loans, they are neither taxable income nor deductible expenses. However, if the S corporation forgives or cancels the shareholder loan, it may be considered a deemed distribution and subject to taxation. It is critical to properly document shareholder loans and treat them as legitimate debts in order for the IRS to recognize them as such.

Shareholder Loan Repayment: When the S corporation repays the shareholder loans, it is not a taxable event for the shareholders. Instead of taxable income, the repayment is treated as a return of the shareholder's capital contribution. However, it is critical to follow proper loan repayment procedures, such as documenting repayment terms and keeping accurate records.

Considerations for Tax Planning: When it comes to shareholder loans, proper tax planning is critical. S corporation owners should ensure that loans are properly structured and documented to support their status as legitimate debt obligations. They can avoid potential tax issues and IRS challenges by doing so. To establish and manage shareholder loans in a way that complies with tax regulations and minimizes tax implications, it is best to consult with a qualified tax professional or accountant.

Understanding the tax implications of shareholder loans and how they are repaid is critical for S corporation owners. Owners can navigate the complexities of shareholder loans and ensure compliance with tax laws while optimizing their overall tax position by following proper procedures and seeking professional advice.

9.5 Techniques for structuring tax-advantaged distributions and debt arrangements

S-corporation distributions can benefit from careful planning and structuring to maximize tax efficiency. This section examines the various strategies available to S corporation owners for structuring tax-efficient distributions and debt arrangements. By implementing these strategies, owners can reduce their tax liabilities while increasing their after-tax income.

1. **Dividends vs. Salary:** S corporation owners have the option of receiving distributions as dividends or salary. Owners can optimize their tax position by carefully balancing the mix of dividends and salary. Dividends have lower tax rates than salary, which are subject to self-employment taxes. It is critical to strike the right balance between personal financial needs and tax efficiency.

2. **Distribution Timing:** Timing is critical for tax-efficient distributions. Owners can reduce their overall tax liability by strategically timing distributions to align with lower tax brackets or taking advantage of tax-saving opportunities in a given year. When determining the timing of distributions, it is critical to consider both personal and business cash flow requirements.

3. **Debt Arrangements:** Debt arrangements can be used as a tax-efficient strategy by S corporations. By properly structuring debt arrangements, owners can deduct interest expenses, lowering taxable income. However, it is critical to

ensure that the debt is genuine, properly documented, and meets the IRS's interest deductibility requirements.

4. **Repayment Plans:** Owners should consider structuring debt repayment plans in a tax-efficient manner when repaying debt. Owners can optimize deductions and cash flow by implementing an appropriate repayment schedule. Working with a qualified tax professional or accountant to create a repayment plan that complies with tax regulations and maximizes tax benefits is critical.

5. **Proportionality in Distribution:** It is critical to ensure that distributions are made in proportion to shareholders' ownership interests. Failure to do so may raise red flags with the IRS, resulting in negative tax consequences. It is critical for compliance and tax efficiency to keep accurate records and document distributions in accordance with ownership percentages.

6. **Professional Advice:** Tax planning can be complicated, and the advice of a qualified tax professional or accountant is invaluable. A professional who specializes in S corporation taxation can assist owners in navigating the complexities of tax-efficient distributions and debt arrangements. They can provide tailored advice based on the specific circumstances of the business and assist in identifying opportunities for tax savings.

S corporation owners can structure their distributions and debt arrangements in a tax-efficient manner, minimizing tax liabilities and maximizing after-tax income, by implementing these strategies. To ensure compliance with tax laws and regulations while optimizing tax efficiency, it is critical to collaborate closely with tax professionals.

9.6 Distribution considerations when liquidating or selling a business

S-corporation owners must carefully consider asset distribution and the tax implications during the process of business liquidation or sale. This section discusses important considerations for distributions during a business liquidation or sale and offers advice on how to optimize tax outcomes.

1. **Understanding the Tax Consequences:** S-corporation owners should be aware of the tax implications of distributions made during the liquidation or sale of a business. Distributions may be treated as ordinary income, capital gains, or a combination of the two, depending on the circumstances. To make informed decisions, it is critical to understand the applicable tax rates and rules.

2. **Evaluating the Distribution Order:** When liquidating or selling a S corporation, owners must determine the distribution order. This decision may have an impact on how the distributions are taxed. Allocating distributions to cover liabilities or obligations first, for example, can help reduce taxable gains. It is best to consult with a tax professional to determine the most tax-efficient distribution strategy.

3. **Capital Losses Can Be Used to Offset Capital Gains From Other Sources:** If the liquidation or sale results in capital losses, S corporation owners can use those losses to offset capital gains from other sources. This can help to lower your overall tax liability. It is critical to understand the rules and limitations governing the use of capital losses, as well as to work with a tax professional to maximize the use of available losses.

4. **Section 338(h)(10) Election:** When selling a business, S corporation owners may consider making a Section 338(h)(10) election. This option treats the transaction as a deemed asset sale for tax purposes, which may result in tax savings. However, this is a complicated choice that necessitates careful consideration and consultation with tax professionals to determine its suitability and potential tax benefits.

5. **Reporting and Compliance:** During the liquidation or sale of a business, proper reporting and compliance with IRS regulations are critical. It is critical to keep accurate records of distribution amounts and tax treatment. Working closely with a tax professional ensures that reporting requirements are met and that potential penalties or scrutiny from tax authorities are avoided.

6. **Seek Professional Advice:** Because of the complexities and potential tax implications of business liquidation or sale, it is strongly advised to consult with a qualified tax professional or accountant. They can offer expert advice tailored to the

individual situation, assisting owners in navigating the distribution process while optimizing tax outcomes.

S corporation owners can make informed decisions that minimize tax liabilities and maximizc financial outcomes by carefully considering distribution considerations during business liquidation or sale. Consulting with tax professionals ensures that tax regulations are followed and that opportunities for tax optimization are identified throughout the liquidation or sale process.

9.7 S corporation distribution compliance with IRS regulations and reporting requirements

When it comes to S-corporation distributions, compliance with IRS regulations and reporting requirements is critical. This section emphasizes the significance of following IRS guidelines while also providing an overview of the key compliance considerations and reporting obligations associated with S corporation distributions.

1. **Proper Classification:** Distributions must be correctly classified as dividends, loans, or other types of transactions based on their nature and purpose. Correctly identifying and documenting the nature of the distribution ensures proper tax treatment and compliance with IRS regulations.

2. **Form 1120S:** S corporations are required to file Form 1120S, U.S. Income Tax Return for a S Corporation, with the IRS. This form reports the S corporation's income, deductions, and distributions. To ensure compliance with IRS requirements, it is critical to accurately report all relevant information, including the amounts and types of distributions.

3. **Shareholder Reporting:** S corporation shareholders receive a Schedule K-1, which reports their share of the S corporation's income, deductions, and distributions. Shareholders must report this information on their individual tax returns, accurately reflecting their S corporation distributions.

4. **Reasonable Compensation:** S corporation owners who are also employees must make certain that they are compensated fairly for their services. The IRS closely monitors this area to ensure that excessive distributions are not labeled as compensation in order to avoid payroll taxes. To comply with IRS guidelines, it is critical to document and report reasonable compensation.

5. **Basis Determination:** Shareholders must keep track of their S corporation basis, which affects the tax treatment of distributions. Accurate basis calculations aid in determining the tax implications of distributions, such as whether they are taxable or not. It is critical for compliance to keep detailed records and use proper basis calculation methods.

6. **Distribution Restrictions:** In some cases, such as accumulated earnings and profits or shareholder agreements, distributions may be restricted. It is critical to adhere to these restrictions and ensure that distributions are in accordance with the applicable rules and agreements.

7. **Qualified Dividends and Capital Gain Distributions:** It is critical to determine whether distributions qualify as qualified

dividends or capital gain distributions when reporting them. Qualified dividends are taxed at a lower rate, whereas capital gain distributions may be taxed differently. Compliance requires proper classification and reporting of these types of distributions.

8. **Documentation and record-keeping:** Accurate and comprehensive documentation is essential for IRS compliance. Maintaining detailed records of distributions, shareholder agreements, basis calculations, and other pertinent information promotes proper reporting and aids in the substantiation of tax positions in the event of IRS inquiries or audits.

9. **Professional Advice:** Given the complexities of IRS regulations and reporting requirements, it is strongly advised to seek professional advice from a qualified tax professional or accountant. They can offer expert advice, ensure IRS compliance, and assist with properly reporting S corporation distributions.

To avoid penalties, IRS scrutiny, and other potential consequences, S corporation distributions must be in accordance with IRS regulations and reporting requirements. S corporation owners can maintain compliance, accurately report distributions, and navigate the complexities of tax compliance with confidence if they understand and fulfill these obligations.

9.8 Real-world examples illustrating the tax implications of various distribution scenarios

This section provides real-world examples of the tax consequences of various S corporation distribution scenarios. These examples show how different distribution decisions can affect the tax liabilities of both the S corporation and its shareholders. S corporation owners can gain a better understanding of the tax implications associated with various distribution strategies by examining these scenarios.

Scenario 1: Equal Dividend Payments

In this case, a S corporation with two equal shareholders decides to pay out profits in the form of dividends. The following example shows how dividend distributions are taxed as ordinary income for shareholders, subject to individual tax rates. It emphasizes the importance of proper reporting and documentation in order to accurately reflect each shareholder's taxable income.

Scenario 2: Proportional Distributions

In this scenario, an S corporation makes distributions to its shareholders in proportion to their ownership percentages. The example shows how the tax implications of these distributions correspond to the shareholders' ownership percentages. It emphasizes the importance of keeping accurate ownership records in order to properly allocate taxable income.

Scenario 3: Return of Capital Distributions

In this example, a S corporation distributes funds to shareholders in the form of a return of capital. Return of capital distributions are generally not taxable, but they do reduce the shareholders' basis in the S corporation. It emphasizes the importance of tracking and adjusting basis calculations as needed.

Scenario 4: Excess Distribution and Capital Gain Treatment

In this scenario, an S corporation distributes more than its accumulated earnings and profits, resulting in an excess distribution. The example shows the tax implications of excessive distributions, including the potential capital gain treatment for shareholders. It emphasizes the importance of understanding the S corporation's accumulated earnings and profits in order to properly report and classify distributions.

Scenario 5: Loan Repayments:

This example examines the tax implications of repaying shareholder loans. It explains how loan repayments are treated as a return of the shareholder's loaned funds rather than taxable distributions. To accurately reflect the tax consequences for both the S corporation and the shareholder, the example emphasizes the importance of distinguishing between loan repayments and taxable distributions.

Conclusion

S corporation owners can gain valuable insights into the tax implications of various distribution scenarios by analyzing these real-life examples. They will have a better understanding of how dividends, proportional distributions, return of capital distributions, excess distributions, and loan repayments are taxed. This knowledge helps to inform distribution decisions, optimize tax planning strategies, and ensure IRS compliance. It is critical to seek personalized advice from a qualified tax professional or accountant based on individual circumstances and the specific distribution scenarios faced by the S corporation.

To make informed decisions, optimize tax efficiency, and ensure compliance with tax laws, owners must understand the complexities of S corporation distributions. This chapter serves as a comprehensive guide, providing valuable insights and guidance on various types of distributions, their tax implications, and effective management strategies.

S corporation owners can properly classify distributions and understand their respective tax treatments by distinguishing between dividends and loans. The distinction between qualified and non-qualified dividends is also important because it determines the preferential tax rates that shareholders are entitled to.

The impact of accumulated earnings and the personal holding company tax on distributions assists owners in navigating the tax implications of retained earnings and avoiding potential tax consequences associated with excessive accumulations.

Understanding the tax implications of shareholder loans and their repayment allows owners to structure debt arrangements in a tax-efficient manner, minimizing taxable income while adhering to IRS regulations.

Implementing tax-efficient distribution and debt-arrangement strategies enables owners to optimize their tax position, reduce tax liabilities, and improve their financial well-being. Owners can effectively manage their tax obligations by considering factors such as distribution timing and structure.

To manage tax implications and maximize after-tax proceeds during business liquidation or sale, distribution strategies must be carefully considered. Proper planning and understanding of tax consequences enable owners to make informed decisions about asset distribution.

For S corporation distributions, compliance with IRS regulations and reporting requirements is critical. Accurate record-keeping, proper documentation, and adherence to reporting guidelines ensure compliance, reduce the risk of audits or penalties, and preserve the tax position of the S corporation.

Real-world examples illustrating the tax consequences of various distribution scenarios provide practical insights into how tax principles are applied. Owners can gain valuable knowledge and apply it to their specific situations by analyzing these examples, facilitating sound decision-making and effective tax planning.

Understanding the nuances of S corporation distributions enables owners to navigate complex tax rules, maximize tax efficiency, and manage their financial affairs effectively. However, it is critical to seek advice from qualified tax professionals or accountants who can provide tailored advice based on your specific circumstances. S corporation owners can successfully navigate the complexities of distributions, minimize tax liabilities, and achieve their financial goals with a thorough understanding and expert assistance.

Chapter 10: How to Deal with the S Corporation Built-In Gains Tax

Introduction

The Built-In Gains (BIG) tax on S corporations is a complex aspect of taxation that S-corporation owners must understand and manage effectively. This chapter delves deeply into the BIG tax, its application to S corporations, and strategies for mitigating its impact through proper planning and restructuring. S corporation owners can optimize their tax position, mitigate potential liabilities, and make informed financial decisions by mastering the nuances of the BIG tax.

Key topics covered in this chapter include:

1. Explanation of the built-in gains tax and its applicability to S corporations.
2. Determining when the BIG tax applies and the triggering events that may lead to its imposition.
3. Calculating and reporting the BIG tax liability.
4. Strategies to minimize or defer the BIG tax through proper planning and restructuring.
5. Utilizing Section 338(h)(10) elections to mitigate the BIG tax consequences.
6. Evaluating the impact of the Tax Cuts and Jobs Act on the BIG tax.
7. Real-life examples illustrating the implications of the BIG tax and effective planning strategies.

8. Compliance considerations and reporting requirements related to the BIG tax.

To summarize, successfully navigating the S Corporation Built-In Gains tax necessitates a thorough understanding of its principles, triggers, calculations, and planning strategies. S corporation owners who understand the nuances of the BIG tax can make informed decisions, optimize their tax position, and effectively manage their financial affairs. Owners can plan their business activities to minimize the impact of the BIG tax if they have a thorough understanding of its applicability and the triggering events that may lead to its imposition.

10.1 An explanation of the built-in gains tax and how it affects S corporations

The built-in gains (BIG) tax is an important consideration for S corporations and influences their tax planning. This section explains the BIG tax, its purpose, and its applicability to S corporations in detail. Understanding the fundamental principles of the BIG tax is critical for S corporation owners in order to successfully navigate its complexities and make sound financial decisions.

The BIG tax is intended to prevent corporations, particularly S corporations, from immediately converting their accumulated C corporation built-in gains into tax-free distributions after converting to S corporation status. Its goal is to ensure that the government collects taxes on gains realized by the corporation prior to its conversion.

When an S corporation has a built-in gain and disposes of the related asset within a certain time frame, the tax becomes applicable. A built-in gain is an increase in the value of an asset that existed when the corporation changed from a C corporation to a S corporation.It may result from a number of things, such as appreciated property, unrealized inventory gains, or other assets with built-in appreciation..

To be eligible for the BIG tax, the corporation must meet certain timing requirements. In general, the tax is triggered if the asset is sold within five years of the S corporation election date. However, the recognition period for certain long-term assets may be extended up to ten years. Understanding these timing rules is critical for business owners who want to assess the potential impact of the BIG tax on their transactions.

The BIG tax is calculated by determining the net recognized built-in gain, which is the excess of the asset's fair market value over its adjusted tax basis. This net recognized built-in gain is subject to corporate taxation at the corporate tax rate. The S corporation's remaining income is taxed at the shareholder level.

Proper planning and restructuring can help reduce or postpone the BIG tax. Owners can optimize their tax position and potentially reduce their BIG tax liabilities by strategically structuring transactions, such as deferring asset sales beyond the recognition period or utilizing tax deferral techniques.

To summarize, the BIG tax is an important consideration for S corporations, and owners must understand its implications. Owners can effectively navigate the BIG tax's complexities by understanding the purpose of the tax, the concept of built-in gains, and the timing rules for triggering the tax. Owners can use this knowledge to make informed decisions, engage in strategic tax planning, and ensure compliance with tax laws. Owners should consult with a qualified tax professional to obtain personalized advice based on their specific circumstances and to fully leverage opportunities to minimize the impact of the BIG tax.

10.2 Determining when the BIG tax applies and the triggering events that may result in its imposition

In this section, we will look at the various scenarios and events that can result in the imposition of the built-in gains (BIG) tax. Understanding these events and their significance is critical for S corporation owners to manage their tax liabilities proactively and effectively plan for the potential application of the BIG tax.

The recognition period is critical in determining whether the BIG tax applies. It begins on the effective date of the S corporation election and lasts for a set period of time, usually five years. However, the recognition period for certain long-term assets may be extended up to ten years. During this time, any disposition of assets with a built-in gain may result in the BIG tax.

Several events can result in the imposition of the BIG tax. The sale, exchange, or transfer of assets that have appreciated in value since the conversion to S corporation status is one of these events. It is important to note that the BIG tax is imposed only on assets that have a built-in gain at the time of the S corporation election and not on all asset sales or transfers.

Several factors must be considered to determine whether a built-in gain is subject to the BIG tax. The asset's fair market value at the time of the S corporation election, as well as its adjusted tax basis, are critical in calculating the potential built-in gain. The BIG tax will be imposed if the net recognized built-in gain exceeds certain thresholds.

During the recognition period, owners must carefully analyze their assets and consider the impact of potential triggering events. Owners can minimize the application of the BIG tax by identifying assets with built-in gains and evaluating the timing and nature of potential dispositions.

Proactive tax planning and restructuring strategies can help mitigate the BIG tax's impact. Techniques such as postponing asset sales beyond the recognition period or utilizing tax deferral methods can effectively reduce or postpone the BIG tax liability.

Understanding the events and factors that led to the imposition of the BIG tax enables S corporation owners to strategically navigate their tax obligations. Owners can optimize their tax position and effectively manage their tax liabilities related to built-in gains by staying informed and engaging in proactive tax planning. It is recommended to consult with a qualified tax professional to obtain personalized advice based on the specific circumstances of the business and to develop tailored strategies for BIG tax mitigation.

10.3 Determining and reporting the MAJOR tax liability

This section contains a comprehensive guide to calculating the built-in gains (BIG) tax liability. To accurately assess and report their BIG tax liability, S corporation owners must understand the calculation process, applicable tax rates, and reporting requirements.

Owners must calculate the BIG tax by determining the recognized built-in gain, which is the difference between the asset's fair market value at the time of the S corporation election and its adjusted tax basis. Multiplying the recognized built-in gain by the relevant BIG tax rate yields the tax liability.

In most cases, the BIG tax rate is the highest corporate tax rate in effect during the recognition period. However, if the S corporation's taxable income falls below a certain threshold, a lower BIG tax rate may apply. To determine the exact applicable tax rate, consult the relevant tax laws and regulations or seek professional advice.

The BIG tax liability must be reported by the owners on their corporate tax return using Form 1120S, U.S. S Corporation Income Tax Return. The BIG tax amount should be reported on the tax return in the Other Taxes section. To ensure compliance with IRS regulations, it is critical to accurately calculate and report the BIG tax liability.

In addition to calculating the tax liability, owners should keep proper documentation and records to support the calculation and reporting of the BIG tax. Keeping records of the fair market value of assets at the time of the S corporation election, adjusted tax basis calculations, and any relevant transactions that trigger the BIG tax are all part of this.

Compliance with reporting requirements is critical in order to avoid penalties and IRS scrutiny. S corporation owners should become acquainted with the specific reporting obligations associated with the BIG tax in order to ensure timely and accurate reporting on their tax returns. Using the services of a qualified tax professional or accountant can help you meet reporting requirements and stay in compliance with tax regulations.

S corporation owners can accurately assess their tax liability and fulfill their compliance responsibilities by understanding the process of calculating the BIG tax liability and fulfilling reporting obligations. Taking the necessary steps to calculate and report the BIG tax accurately will assist in ensuring compliance with IRS regulations and avoiding potential penalties.

10.4 Strategies for avoiding or postponing the BIG tax through careful planning and restructuring

This section delves into the strategies that S corporation owners can use to reduce or postpone the built-in gains (BIG) tax through proactive planning and restructuring. Owners can optimize their tax position and potentially reduce their tax liabilities associated with the BIG tax by implementing these strategies.

Consider asset sales rather than stock sales as one effective strategy. Owners may be able to allocate the purchase price to the assets themselves by structuring a transaction as an asset sale rather than a stock sale, potentially reducing the recognized built-in gain subject to the BIG tax. Proper asset valuation and consultation with tax professionals can assist in optimizing the allocation of the purchase price and minimizing the BIG tax impact.

Entity conversions are another effective strategy. Owners can reset the recognition period for built-in gains by converting the S corporation to another entity type, such as a C corporation. This conversion can help mitigate the significant tax consequences of pre-existing built-in gains. However, to ensure the desired outcome, it is critical to carefully evaluate the potential trade-offs and tax implications of entity conversions and consult with tax advisors.

Tax deferral strategies can be used to postpone the recognition of built-in gains, potentially reducing the immediate tax impact. Techniques such as installment sales, like-kind exchanges, and the use of tax deferral vehicles such as Qualified Opportunity Zones can postpone the recognition of gains and give you more time to plan for the BIG tax consequences. These strategies enable owners to postpone their tax liability while maintaining financial flexibility.

It's important to remember that each strategy has its own set of considerations and potential limitations. To determine the best strategy for their situation, owners should carefully evaluate their specific circumstances and consult with tax professionals. Proper planning and restructuring can help owners reduce or postpone the BIG tax, giving them greater control over their tax liabilities and potential tax savings.

S corporation owners can optimize their tax position, mitigate the impact of the BIG tax, and potentially reduce their overall tax liabilities by implementing these strategies and exploring the available options. Engaging the services of qualified tax professionals or advisors can provide invaluable assistance in selecting and implementing the most effective strategies tailored to individual circumstances.

10.5 Utilizing Section 338(h)(10) elections to reduce the BIG tax consequences

In this section, we will look at the advantages and disadvantages of using Section 338(h)(10) elections as a valuable tool for mitigating the effects of the built-in gains (BIG) tax. Understanding the mechanics of this election, as well as its requirements and potential tax savings, is critical for S corporation owners looking to effectively manage their BIG tax liabilities.

Section 338(h)(10) elections permit a purchasing corporation to treat a S corporation acquisition as a deemed asset purchase for tax purposes. This option allows the purchasing corporation to increase the tax basis of acquired assets to their fair market value, effectively eliminating potential built-in gains that would otherwise be subject to the BIG tax.

The purchasing corporation can reduce the recognized built-in gain by electing to allocate the purchase price to the underlying assets under Section 338(h)(10). This option allows the acquiring corporation to increase the tax basis of the assets, potentially resulting in future tax savings when the assets are sold or depreciated.

It is important to note, however, that Section 338(h)(10) elections have specific requirements and considerations. These include obtaining the consent of all S corporation shareholders, adhering to strict timelines, and adhering to IRS regulations. Furthermore, the purchasing corporation must meet the eligibility requirements for making the election.

Owners considering Section 338(h)(10) elections should carefully consider their specific circumstances, such as the nature of the S corporation's assets and potential future business plans. Using the expertise of tax professionals or advisors who have experience with such elections can provide invaluable guidance while also ensuring compliance with the necessary requirements.

Section 338(h)(10) elections can provide significant tax benefits by mitigating the large tax consequences of recognizing built-in gains. Owners can potentially reduce their tax liabilities and improve their overall tax efficiency by increasing the tax basis of acquired assets. However, to determine the suitability and feasibility of this option in individual cases, it is critical to thoroughly analyze the implications and consult with qualified professionals.

Understanding the opportunities presented by Section 338(h)(10) elections, as well as their potential to reduce the BIG tax consequences, is a valuable tool for owners looking to proactively manage their tax liabilities and optimize their overall tax position.

10.6 Evaluating the Tax Cuts and Jobs Act's impact on the BIG tax

This section examines how the Tax Cuts and Jobs Act (TCJA) affected the built-in gains (BIG) tax. The Tax Cuts and Jobs Act (TCJA), enacted in 2017, made significant changes to the tax code that can affect the BIG tax calculations and considerations. Understanding these changes is critical for S corporation owners in order to plan for the BIG tax and make informed decisions.

The TCJA made a significant change by lowering the corporate tax rate. Because the tax rate used to calculate the tax liability on built-in gains is based on the corporate tax rate in effect during the recognition period, the lower corporate tax rate can affect the calculation of the BIG tax. The lower corporate tax rate may result in lower tax liabilities for built-in gains recognized after the TCJA's enactment.

Furthermore, the TCJA altered the net operating loss (NOL) provisions. NOLs can no longer be carried back to previous years under the TCJA, and the deduction for NOLs is limited to 80% of taxable income. These changes may affect the use of NOLs to offset built-in gains as well as the timing and amount of the BIG tax liability.

The TCJA also changed the way business interest expense deductions are treated. The business interest expense limitation, also known as the limitation on business interest deductions, can affect the amount of interest expense that can be deducted for tax purposes. This restriction may have an impact on the calculation of the BIG tax for S corporations with significant interest expense associated with built-in gains.

Furthermore, Section 199A of the TCJA established a deduction for qualified business income (QBI). This deduction allows eligible taxpayers to deduct up to 20% of their qualified business income earned through pass-through entities such as S corporations. The availability and use of the QBI deduction can have an impact on S corporation owners' overall tax liability, including any BIG tax obligations.

It is critical for S corporation owners to stay informed about the TCJA's changes and their potential impact on the BIG tax. To ensure accurate calculations and compliance with the updated regulations, consult with qualified tax professionals or advisors.

Owners can adapt their tax planning strategies and optimize their tax position by evaluating the impact of the TCJA on the BIG tax. Understanding the TCJA's changes helps owners stay current on the evolving tax landscape and make informed decisions to effectively manage the

10.7 Real-life examples illustrating the implications of the BIG tax and effective planning strategies

In this section, we present real-world examples of the implications of the built-in gains (BIG) tax as well as effective planning strategies to mitigate its impact. These scenarios illustrate various scenarios and provide practical insights into how the BIG tax can occur and how owners can use strategic measures to reduce their tax liabilities.

Example 1: Appreciated Asset Sale

ABC Inc. is a limited liability company that owns valuable real estate. ABC Inc. decides to sell the property after holding it for several years. However, since its acquisition, the property has appreciated significantly, resulting in a built-in gain. This built-in gain could trigger the BIG tax if not properly planned for.

In this case, ABC Inc. consults with tax advisors to structure the transaction in the most tax-efficient way possible. They are thinking about using the Section 338(h)(10) election, which treats the sale as if it were a sale of assets by the corporation and then liquidation. ABC Inc. can increase the tax basis of its assets and potentially reduce the BIG tax liability by making this election.

Example 2: Asset Sale Timing

XYZ Corp. is an S corporation with built-in gains from asset sales. Because of these gains, they anticipate a significant increase in their taxable income for the current year. They do, however, have the option of deferring the recognition of the gains to a later year.

In this case, XYZ Corp. considers its overall tax situation and decides to postpone the recognition of built-in gains by strategically timing asset sales. They can reduce the impact of the BIG tax and potentially benefit from lower tax rates in future years by spreading out the sales over multiple years.

These examples emphasize the importance of understanding the BIG tax's implications and implementing effective planning strategies. S corporation owners can identify opportunities for tax optimization and mitigate the impact of the BIG tax on their business operations and financial outcomes by working closely with tax professionals.

It is critical to remember that each situation is unique, and the strategies used will vary depending on the circumstances. It is strongly advised to consult with qualified tax advisors or professionals to ensure accurate analysis, personalized advice, and compliance with applicable tax laws.

S corporation owners can gain valuable insights and apply these lessons to their own tax planning efforts by examining real-life examples and understanding the strategies used to address the BIG tax. Effective planning and proactive measures can assist owners in optimizing their tax position, minimizing their BIG tax liabilities, and improving their overall financial well-being

10.8 BIG tax compliance considerations and reporting requirements

In this section, we emphasize the importance of compliance considerations and reporting requirements associated with the built-in gains (BIG) tax. To ensure compliance with Internal Revenue Service (IRS) regulations, S corporation owners must understand and fulfill their obligations. Owners can reduce the risk of audits, penalties, and other potential issues by adhering to these requirements while maintaining the integrity of their tax position.

Accurate Record-Keeping: When it comes to the BIG tax, keeping accurate and detailed records is critical. To accurately determine built-in gains and losses, owners should keep track of relevant transactions, such as asset acquisition and disposition. Clear and comprehensive records serve as supporting documentation in the event of IRS audits or inquiries.

Proper Documentation: Along with accurate record-keeping, proper documentation is required to substantiate any BIG tax transactions, elections, or restructuring strategies. This includes keeping records of Section 338(h)(10) elections, asset valuations, and any other documents that demonstrate compliance with tax regulations.

Adherence to Reporting Guidelines: S corporation owners must follow the IRS's reporting guidelines. This includes submitting the necessary tax forms, such as Form 1120S, U.S. Income Tax Return for a S Corporation, and Schedule M-3, Net Income (Loss) Reconciliation for Corporations with $10 Million or More in Total Assets. It is critical to report built-in gains accurately, calculate the BIG tax liability, and disclose any relevant information required by the IRS.

Consultation with Tax Professionals: Due to the complexities of the BIG tax and its associated compliance requirements, it is strongly advised to seek guidance from qualified tax professionals or advisors. These experts can help you navigate the reporting requirements, ensure accurate calculations, and provide personalized advice based on your specific circumstances.

S corporation owners can reduce the risk of IRS scrutiny, penalties, and potential legal complications by prioritizing compliance considerations and meeting reporting requirements related to the BIG tax. Accurate record-keeping, proper documentation, and consultation with tax professionals are critical components of maintaining compliance and protecting the business's financial stability.

It is important to note that tax laws and regulations can and will change over time, and it is the responsibility of S corporation owners to stay up-to-date on any updates or changes to the reporting requirements. Owners can navigate the complexities of the BIG tax with confidence and ensure ongoing compliance with IRS regulations by staying proactive and up-to-date with the evolving tax landscape.

Conclusion

To summarize, successfully navigating the S Corporation Built-In Gains tax necessitates a thorough understanding of its principles, triggers, calculations, and planning strategies. S corporation owners can make informed decisions, optimize their tax position, and effectively manage their financial affairs if they understand the nuances of the BIG tax. Owners can plan their business activities to minimize the impact of the BIG tax if they have a thorough understanding of its applicability and the triggering events that may lead to its imposition.

To ensure compliance with tax regulations, it is critical to accurately calculate and report the BIG tax liability. Owners can confidently determine their BIG tax liability and fulfill their reporting obligations by following the step-by-step guide provided in this chapter, reducing the risk of errors or penalties.

Strategic planning and restructuring are important in minimizing or deferring the BIG tax. Owners can optimize their tax position and potentially reduce their BIG tax liabilities by implementing appropriate techniques such as asset sales, entity conversions, or tax deferral strategies.

The Section 338(h)(10) election is a powerful tool available to S corporation owners. Understanding the mechanics and requirements of this option enables owners to assess its suitability for mitigating the effects of the BIG tax. Owners may achieve significant tax savings and better manage their tax liabilities by making this election.

The Tax Cuts and Jobs Act has altered the tax landscape, including the implementation of the BIG tax. It is critical for S corporation owners to be aware of and understand these changes. Owners can adjust their planning strategies accordingly and ensure they are taking advantage of any available tax benefits by staying up-to-date with the tax code.

This chapter includes real-life examples to demonstrate the implications of the BIG tax and effective planning strategies. These examples depict various scenarios and show how proper planning can reduce the tax consequences. Analyzing these examples can provide owners with valuable insights and practical guidance as they navigate the complexities of the BIG tax.

When dealing with the BIG tax, it is critical to comply with IRS regulations and reporting requirements. Accurate record-keeping, proper documentation, and following reporting guidelines all help to ensure compliance and reduce the risk of audits or penalties. Owners can confidently manage their large tax obligations if they maintain compliance.

Finally, understanding and navigating the S Corporation Built-In Gains tax is critical for S corporation owners. Owners can optimize their tax position, minimize liabilities, and make informed financial decisions by understanding the BIG tax's principles, triggers, calculations, planning strategies, and compliance requirements. It is recommended that owners consult with a qualified tax professional to obtain personalized advice based on their specific circumstances and fully capitalize on the BIG tax opportunities.

Chapter 11: Considerations and Consequences of S Corporation Election and Termination

Introduction

The decision to elect or terminate S corporation status can have serious consequences for small business owners. This chapter examines the considerations and consequences of electing S corporation status or terminating S corporation status, empowering owners to make informed decisions that align with their business goals and tax strategies.

Key topics covered in this chapter include:

1. Understanding the advantages and disadvantages of S corporation status.
2. Eligibility criteria and requirements for making an S corporation election.
3. Evaluating the tax implications of an S corporation election on business income, distributions, and payroll taxes.
4. Strategic considerations for determining the optimal time to make an S corporation election.
5. Consequences of terminating S corporation status and reverting to a C corporation or other entity type.
6. Assessing the tax implications of S corporation termination, including built-in gains tax and loss limitations.
7. Navigating the IRS processes and deadlines for S corporation elections and terminations.

8. Real-life case studies illustrating the impact of S corporation elections and terminations on tax outcomes.

By understanding the considerations and consequences of S corporation elections and terminations, business owners can make informed decisions that align with their long-term goals and tax strategies.

11.1 Understanding the advantages and disadvantages of S corporation status

This section provides a comprehensive overview of the benefits and drawbacks of S corporation status. Understanding these factors is critical for business owners to make informed decisions about the structure of their entity. Let's go over the main points in depth:

Advantages of S-corporation status:

1. **Pass-through taxation:** The pass-through tax structure of an S corporation is a significant advantage. Profits and losses are passed through to shareholders, who report them on their personal tax returns. This avoids the double taxation that occurs with C corporations, which tax both the corporation and its shareholders.

2. **Limited liability protection:** S corporations, like other corporate structures, provide shareholders with limited liability protection. This means that shareholders' personal assets are generally protected from the company's liabilities and debts. Legal action or business debts rarely pose a threat to personal assets, such as homes and savings.

3. **Potential tax savings:** S corporations offer the possibility of tax savings. S corporations, unlike C corporations, are not subject to corporate income tax. This can result in tax savings, especially for businesses with large profits. Furthermore, S corporations permit shareholders to avoid self-employment taxes on their share of business income as long as they are fairly compensated.

Disadvantages of S-corporation status:

1. **Ownership restrictions:** S corporations have stringent eligibility and ownership requirements. S corporations, for example, cannot have more than 100 shareholders, and certain types of shareholders, such as non-resident aliens and other corporations, are not permitted. These constraints can make it difficult to raise capital or expand ownership.

2. **Limited flexibility in allocating profits and losses:** S corporations have limited flexibility in allocating profits and losses to shareholders based on their ownership percentage. This allocation is generally proportional to the shareholders' investment in the business, which limits the flexibility in distributing profits differently based on individual circumstances.

3. **Compliance requirements:** S corporations must comply with ongoing compliance requirements, such as holding regular shareholder and director meetings, keeping accurate financial records, and filing annual reports with the state. When

compared to other business structures, these administrative responsibilities can add complexity and administrative burden.

Understanding the benefits and drawbacks of S corporation status allows business owners to weigh the benefits against the drawbacks and determine if it meets their specific needs and goals. To determine the suitability of S corporation status based on individual circumstances, consult with a qualified tax professional or legal advisor.

11.2 Eligibility criteria and S corporation election requirements

This section delves into the requirements and eligibility criteria for making an S corporation election. Understanding these criteria and procedural requirements is critical for businesses interested in obtaining S corporation status. Let's go over the main points in depth:

1. **Number and type of shareholders:** A company must have 100 shareholders or less to qualify for S corporation status. Individuals, estates, certain trusts, and tax-exempt organizations can all be shareholders. Non-resident aliens, partnerships, and the vast majority of corporations are ineligible shareholders.

2. **Shareholder restrictions:** S corporations have specific ownership restrictions. S corporations, for example, cannot have shareholders who are non-resident aliens, partnerships, or most other types of corporations. These restrictions are in

place to protect the S corporation's status as a closely held entity.

3. **Timing and Form 2553 submission:** To elect S corporation status, the company must submit Form 2553, Election by a Small Business Corporation, to the IRS. The business must file this form within the first two months and fifteen days of the tax year in which it wishes to be treated as an S corporation. Alternatively, if the company meets certain requirements, it can file Form 2553 in the previous tax year.

4. **Meeting IRS requirements:** In order to qualify for S corporation status, the company must meet additional IRS requirements in addition to filing Form 2553. This includes making certain that all shareholders agree to the election, keeping accurate records of shareholder allocations, and meeting ongoing compliance requirements.

Businesses must carefully review and meet the eligibility criteria and requirements for electing an S corporation. Failure to meet these requirements, or miss the filing deadline may result in the loss of S corporation status and the tax benefits that come with it. To ensure compliance with the eligibility criteria and procedural requirements for an S corporation election, it is best to consult with a qualified tax professional or legal advisor.

11.3 Evaluating the tax implications of an S corporation election on business income, distributions, and payroll taxes

In this section, we look at how a S corporation election affects the taxation of various aspects of the business, such as income taxation, distributions, and payroll taxes. Understanding these tax considerations is critical for business owners thinking about forming a S corporation. Let's go over the main points in depth:

1. **Pass-through taxation:** One of the primary benefits of S corporation status is the structure of pass-through taxation. Unlike C corporations, which are taxed twice (once at the corporate level and again at the individual level for shareholders), S corporations pass through their income, deductions, and credits to the shareholders' personal tax returns. This enables shareholders to report their portion of the S corporation's income and pay taxes at their individual rates.

2. **Potential tax savings from reasonable compensation:** When operating as a S corporation, business owners have the option of allocating a portion of the business income to themselves as reasonable compensation. As a result, the company's taxable income may be reduced, resulting in lower overall tax liabilities. To avoid IRS scrutiny, it is critical to ensure that the compensation is reasonable and in line with industry standards.

3. **Implications for self-employment taxes:** In contrast to sole proprietorships and partnerships, where all income is subject to self-employment taxes, owners of S corporation may be able to reduce their self-employment tax liability. Distributions and other types of income may be exempt from self-employment taxes, but only the portion of income allocated as reasonable compensation is subject to them. For business owners, this can result in significant tax savings.

4. **Payroll taxes and compliance:** Owners who are also employees of an S corporation must pay themselves a reasonable salary and withhold payroll taxes accordingly. Noncompliance with payroll tax obligations can result in penalties and potential IRS audits. To avoid any tax-related issues, it is critical to understand the payroll tax requirements and ensure proper compliance.

Owners can assess the potential tax savings and overall tax burden by carefully evaluating the tax implications of a S corporation election on business income, distributions, and payroll taxes. However, it is critical to seek personalized advice from a qualified tax professional or accountant based on the specific circumstances of the business. This will help to ensure tax law compliance and maximize the tax benefits associated with S corporation status.

11.4 Strategic considerations for determining the best time to form a S corporation

Determining the best time to form an S corporation necessitates careful consideration of a number of strategic factors. This section delves into these factors to assist business owners in making informed decisions. Let's look at the main points:

1. **Business profitability and projected income:** Before deciding on an S corporation, it is critical to evaluate the company's profitability and projected income. S-corporation status is generally more advantageous for businesses that generate significant profits. An S corporation election may not be advantageous from a tax standpoint if the business is currently operating at a loss or is not expected to generate significant income in the near future. Evaluating the company's profitability and growth potential will aid in determining the best time to hold the election.

2. **Long-term goals and exit strategy:** When determining the best time for an S corporation election, long-term goals must be considered. If the company intends to expand, attract investors, or change its ownership structure, the timing of the election must be coordinated with these objectives. Furthermore, if the company intends to sell or transfer ownership, it may be advantageous to establish S corporation status well in advance to maximize potential tax advantages during the transition.

3. **Coordination with other business events:** It is critical to time the S corporation election in conjunction with other significant business events. For example, if the company is planning a large investment, acquisition, or restructuring, the S corporation election may be advantageous. Coordinating the timing ensures that the election is in line with the overall business strategy and reduces the likelihood of disruptions or complications.

4. **Compliance with IRS timelines:** The IRS has specific timelines and requirements for making a S corporation election. It is critical to understand and adhere to these deadlines in order for the election to be valid. In most cases, the election must be made by the 15th day of the third month of the tax year in which the election is to take effect. Failure to meet these deadlines may result in S corporation status being delayed or denied, with potential tax consequences. To ensure compliance with IRS timelines, careful planning and coordination with tax professionals or accountants are required.

Owners can strategically determine the best time to make an S corporation election by considering the company's profitability, projected income, long-term goals, and coordinating the election with other business events. It is recommended that qualified professionals be consulted in order to assess the specific circumstances of the business and obtain personalized advice. This will help maximize potential tax benefits while minimizing disruptions during the transition to S corporation status.

11.5 Consequences of losing S corporation status and converting to C corporation or another entity type

Changing from an S corporation to a C corporation or another entity type has a number of consequences that business owners should carefully consider. This section delves into these consequences in order to provide a comprehensive understanding. Let us look at the main points:

1. **Tax consequences:** One of the most significant consequences of terminating S corporation status is the potential tax consequences. When a business converts from an S corporation to a C corporation or another entity type, it may be subject to new tax rules and rates. For example, C corporations are subject to double taxation, which means that both the corporation's income and shareholder dividends are taxed. This change in tax treatment may have an impact on the company's and its owners' overall tax liability. To make informed decisions, it is critical to assess the potential tax consequences and consult with tax professionals or accountants.

2. **Changes in ownership structure:** When a S corporation's status is terminated, the business's ownership structure may change. The termination may include the conversion of shares or the transfer of ownership interests, depending on the circumstances. It's critical to think about the legal and contractual implications of these changes, such as any buy-sell agreements, shareholder agreements, or obligations to existing shareholders. To ensure a smooth and legally valid

transition, proper documentation and compliance with legal requirements are required.

3. **Legal considerations:** Terminating S corporation status entails legal issues that must be carefully addressed. Legal formalities, filings, or approvals may be required to effect the termination, depending on the jurisdiction and the specific circumstances of the business. To ensure compliance with all necessary legal requirements and procedures, it is best to consult with legal professionals who specialize in business law.

4. **Changes in operations and administration:** Converting to a C corporation or another entity type may necessitate operational and administrative changes. Accounting methods may need to be adjusted, corporate governance structures revised, or additional regulatory requirements met. Owners should consider the practical implications of these changes, as well as the potential impact on the day-to-day operations and administrative responsibilities of the business.

It is critical for business owners to carefully consider the implications of losing their S corporation status and converting to a C corporation or another entity type. Potential tax implications, changes in ownership structure, legal requirements, and operational adjustments should all be considered. To navigate this process effectively and make informed decisions that align with the business's goals and long-term strategy, consulting with professionals such as tax advisors, attorneys, and accountants is highly recommended.

11.6 Evaluating the tax implications of S corporation dissolution, including built-in gains tax and loss limitations

When considering the termination of S corporation status, it is critical to consider the potential tax consequences, including the application of built-in gains tax and loss limitations. This section delves into the tax implications to provide a thorough understanding. Let's look at the main points:

1. **Built-in gains tax:** When an S corporation's status is terminated, the business may be subject to the built-in gains tax (BIG tax). The BIG tax is intended to discourage businesses from converting from C to S corporation status solely to avoid paying taxes on built-in gains. Built-in gains are the increases in the value of assets held by the S corporation when it was converted from a C corporation. If the company sells these assets within a certain time frame, the built-in gains are subject to the BIG tax. Understanding the BIG tax's potential application is critical for owners planning for and managing the tax consequences of terminating S corporation status.

2. **Loss limitations:** The loss of S corporation status may have implications for the use of net operating losses (NOLs). NOLs are created when a company's deductions exceed its taxable income, causing a loss. S corporations are subject to certain limitations on the use of NOLs, which may vary depending on the jurisdiction's specific tax laws and regulations. These NOL limitations may change if S corporation status is terminated,

potentially affecting the business's ability to offset future taxable income with NOLs. It is critical to assess the impact of NOL limitations in order to understand the potential impact on the business's tax position following termination.

Understanding the tax implications of S corporation termination is critical for business owners, including the potential application of built-in gains tax and loss limitations. Owners can plan effectively and make informed decisions about the termination of S corporation status by assessing these implications. To navigate the complexities of these tax consequences and ensure compliance with relevant tax laws and regulations, consulting with tax professionals or accountants with expertise in corporate taxation is highly recommended.

11.7 Navigating the IRS processes and deadlines for S corporation elections and terminations

To ensure compliance and timely completion of necessary filings, it is critical to navigate the IRS processes and deadlines for S corporation elections and terminations. We provide guidance on the key aspects of this process in this section. Let us investigate further:

S corporation election

To make an S corporation election, business owners must file Form 2553, Election by a Small Business Corporation, with the IRS. The deadline for submitting this form is typically two and a half months after the start of the tax year in which the election is to take effect. It is critical to meet the deadline in order for the election to be processed on time. Additionally, certain eligibility requirements and ownership restrictions must be met in order to qualify for S corporation status. Understanding these requirements and gathering the necessary information is critical for a successful S corporation election process.

S corporation termination

When considering the termination of S corporation status, it is critical to understand the IRS processes and deadlines involved. To terminate S corporation status, the company must generally file Form 966, Corporate Dissolution or Liquidation, with the IRS. The termination must be reported to the IRS within 30 days of its effective date. It is critical that this reporting deadline be met in order to avoid any potential penalties or complications. Other legal and regulatory requirements may also apply, depending on the circumstances and jurisdiction in which the business operates. To ensure compliance with all relevant regulations and procedures, it is recommended that you consult with legal and tax professionals.

Business owners can effectively navigate these procedures by understanding the IRS processes and deadlines for S corporation elections and terminations. It is critical to ensure that all required forms are filed on time and accurately, that deadlines are met, and that all eligibility criteria and restrictions are met in order to achieve the desired tax status and avoid potential complications. Engaging the services of experienced tax professionals or legal counsel can provide valuable guidance and assistance throughout the process, assisting business owners in navigating the complexities of IRS compliance and achieving their desired outcomes.

11.8 Case studies from real life demonstrating the impact of S corporation elections and terminations on tax outcomes

Real-world case studies shed light on the practical implications of S corporation elections and terminations on tax outcomes. Business owners can gain a better understanding of how different scenarios can result in different tax consequences by looking at these examples. Let us look at some examples of case studies:

Case Study 1: S Corporation Election

Company X, a small business with steady growth, decides to form a S corporation in order to benefit from pass-through taxation. By electing S corporation status, the owners can avoid corporate double taxation and have business income flow directly to their personal tax returns. This case study demonstrates how the S corporation election can result in substantial tax savings for the owners, allowing them to keep more of their earnings and invest in business growth.

Case Study 2: S Corporation Election Timing

Company Y was a sole proprietorship for several years before experiencing a profit surge. The owners carefully consider the timing of their S corporation election, taking into account factors such as projected income, tax rates, and long-term objectives. They can maximize their tax savings and align the conversion with other business events, such as the hiring of additional employees, by strategically timing the election. This case study demonstrates how, with proper planning and timing, the benefits of an S corporation election can be maximized.

Case Study 3: Termination and Inheritance Tax

Company Z, a S corporation, decides to drop its S corporation status and convert to a C corporation in order to take advantage of new investment opportunities. However, this decision results in the recognition of built-in gains, which may result in tax liabilities. The owners carefully consider the implications of terminating S corporation status, taking into account the impact of built-in gains tax and loss limitations. This case study emphasizes the importance of considering the tax implications before terminating S corporation status.

Business owners can gain practical insights into the impact of S corporation elections and terminations on tax outcomes by reviewing these real-life case studies. Each scenario illustrates the distinct considerations and consequences associated with various decisions. Understanding these examples enables owners to make informed decisions, tailor their strategies to their specific circumstances, and manage their tax positions effectively.

Please keep in mind that the case studies provided are only for illustration purposes and should not be construed as specific tax advice. It is strongly advised to seek personalized advice from qualified tax professionals or advisors based on individual circumstances.

Conclusion

Chapter 11 has provided a thorough examination of the factors and consequences involved with S corporation elections and terminations. Understanding these factors allows business owners to make informed decisions that are in line with their long-term objectives and tax strategies.

We've looked at the benefits and drawbacks of S corporation status, the eligibility criteria and requirements for making a S corporation election, and the tax implications for business income, distributions, and payroll taxes throughout this chapter. We've also talked about the strategic factors to consider when deciding when to make an S corporation election and the consequences of terminating S corporation status.

Furthermore, we investigated the tax implications of S corporation termination, including the possible application of built-in gains tax and loss limitations. We have provided advice on how to navigate the IRS processes and deadlines for S corporation elections and terminations, emphasizing the importance of compliance and timely filings. Real-world case studies have also demonstrated the impact of S corporation elections and terminations on tax outcomes, providing practical insights into the decision-making process.

By applying what they've learned in this chapter, business owners will be able to make well-informed decisions about their S corporation status. They can weigh the benefits and drawbacks, calculate the tax implications, and plan their elections or terminations strategically. This knowledge enables owners to align their business structure with their long-term goals, maximize tax savings, and stay in compliance with IRS regulations.

It is important to note that the information in this chapter is provided solely for educational purposes and should not be construed as legal or tax advice. Each company's circumstances are unique, so consulting with qualified professionals to tailor strategies to specific situations is recommended.

Using the knowledge gained in this chapter, business owners can confidently navigate the complexities of S corporation elections and terminations, ensuring their decisions align with their overall business objectives and tax strategies.

Chapter 12: S Corporation Audits and IRS Compliance

Introduction

In the ever-changing landscape of tax regulations, S corporation owners must prioritize compliance with IRS requirements and be ready for potential audits. This chapter is a comprehensive guide that provides an in-depth overview of S corporation audits, IRS compliance requirements, and effective strategies for mitigating audit risks and successfully navigating the audit process.

Understanding the triggers and selection criteria for S corporation audits, maintaining accurate and organized financial records to support IRS compliance, evaluating the different types of IRS audits and their scope, strategies for minimizing audit risks through proper reporting and documentation, preparing for a S corporation audit by gathering supporting documentation and engaging professional assistance, and navigating the audit process are among the key topics covered in this chapter. Proactive measures to reduce the likelihood of future audits and improve compliance are also discussed.

This chapter empowers S corporation owners to safeguard their businesses, mitigate penalties, and maintain financial stability by providing them with the necessary knowledge and strategies to navigate IRS compliance requirements and manage audit risks. It provides valuable insights into the IRS audit process, emphasizing the importance of maintaining accurate records, thorough documentation, and adhering to reporting guidelines.

It is critical to note that the information in this chapter is provided solely for educational purposes and should not be construed as legal or tax advice. Because each company's circumstances are unique, seeking advice from qualified professionals is recommended to ensure compliance with IRS regulations and tailored strategies for specific situations.

By prioritizing IRS compliance and implementing effective audit risk mitigation strategies, S corporation owners can proactively protect their businesses, maintain trust with tax authorities, and confidently navigate the audit process. This chapter is a valuable resource for owners who want to better understand IRS compliance requirements and manage the complexities of S corporation audits.

12.1 Understanding the S corporation audit triggers and selection criteria

In this section, we hope to provide a thorough understanding of the triggers and selection criteria for S corporation audits. It is critical for S corporation owners to understand the factors that may increase the likelihood of an audit. Understanding these triggers allows business owners to address potential areas of concern and take appropriate measures to reduce audit risks.

To identify S corporations that are more likely to be audited, the IRS employs a variety of selection criteria. While the IRS does not disclose the specific selection process, certain factors have been identified as potential triggers for S corporation audits. Inconsistent reporting, such as differences in income, deductions, or shareholder distributions, can attract the IRS's attention. Large deductions or unusual items reported on the tax return may also raise suspicion, especially if they differ significantly from industry norms or prior-year filings.

Significant changes in financials, such as a sharp increase in revenues or expenses, can raise IRS red flags. Furthermore, the IRS may target S corporations that conduct transactions with related parties, as these transactions may necessitate more scrutiny to ensure compliance with the arm's length principle.

Understanding these triggers is critical for S-corporation owners because it allows them to be proactive in dealing with potential issues. Owners can reduce the likelihood of an audit by reviewing their financial records, conducting internal audits, and ensuring the accuracy and consistency of their tax filings.

Furthermore, proper documentation is required to substantiate the items reported on the tax return. Maintaining organized and accurate financial records, such as receipts, invoices, and supporting documentation for deductions and shareholder distributions, can assist in demonstrating the legitimacy of reported figures and mitigating audit risks.

Business owners can take a proactive approach to ensuring compliance with IRS regulations and minimizing audit risks by becoming familiar with the triggers and selection criteria for S corporation audits. Taking the necessary steps to keep accurate records, consistently report income and deductions, and address any potential red flags will not only reduce the likelihood of an audit, but will also help build trust with the IRS.

While understanding the triggers for S corporation audits is beneficial, it does not guarantee immunity from audits. The IRS conducts audits based on a variety of factors, and even businesses with no obvious triggers may be chosen for scrutiny. As a result, regardless of their audit risk profile, all S corporation owners should prioritize compliance and sound record-keeping practices.

S corporation owners can reduce the disruption and potential financial impact of an IRS audit by remaining vigilant, addressing potential triggers, and maintaining accurate records. The information in this section serves as a starting point for understanding the triggers and selection criteria for S corporation audits, allowing owners to take proactive measures to improve compliance and reduce audit risks.

12.2 Keeping accurate and well-organized financial records to ensure IRS compliance

In this section, we emphasize the importance of keeping accurate and well-organized financial records to support IRS compliance. Maintaining meticulous and well-organized records is critical for S corporation owners because it establishes the credibility and accuracy of their financial information, ensures smooth IRS compliance, and minimizes potential issues during audits or inquiries.

The foundation for keeping accurate financial records is proper bookkeeping practices. This includes promptly and accurately recording all business transactions and using dependable accounting software or systems to track income, expenses, and other financial activities. To provide a clear and transparent picture of the business's financial activities, each transaction should be properly classified and documented.

There must be supporting documentation for all income, expenses, and deductions listed on the tax return. Invoices, receipts, bank statements, sales records, purchase orders, and contracts are examples of such documentation. S corporation owners can substantiate the amounts reported on their tax returns and provide evidence of the legitimacy of their financial transactions by keeping these records.

In addition to transaction records, the S corporation must keep track of shareholder distributions, loans, and other financial transactions. These records should clearly document the purpose, amounts, and terms of these transactions, ensuring IRS compliance and demonstrating proper fund allocation within the business.

Owners should also ensure that their financial records are well-organized and easily accessible. Establishing a logical filing system for both physical and digital records, allowing for efficient retrieval and review when needed, is part of this. Proper financial record organization allows owners to respond quickly to IRS inquiries or requests for documentation, saving time and minimizing potential disruptions to their business operations.

S corporation owners can effectively support IRS compliance efforts by keeping accurate and organized financial records. Having thorough documentation readily available in the event of an audit or inquiry enables owners to respond to IRS inquiries quickly and demonstrate the accuracy and legitimacy of their financial reporting.

It should be noted that the retention period for financial records varies depending on the nature of the transaction and applicable laws. To ensure compliance with record retention requirements, it is best to consult with a tax professional or review IRS guidelines.

Finally, keeping accurate and organized financial records is critical for S corporation owners seeking IRS compliance. Owners can establish the credibility and accuracy of their financial information by implementing sound bookkeeping practices, retaining necessary documentation, and organizing records in a systematic manner. This not only speeds up the IRS compliance process, but it also instills trust in the company's financial operations and strengthens its overall compliance efforts.

12.3 Assessing the various types of IRS audits and their scope

In this section, we look at the different types of IRS audits that S corporation owners may face, as well as an overview of their scope and procedures. Understanding the various types of audits is critical for S corporation owners because it allows them to adequately prepare for and navigate the audit process.

1. Correspondence audits:

The most common type of IRS audit for S corporations is a correspondence audit, also known as a mail audit. Typically, these audits involve a review of specific items on the tax return or a request for additional documentation to support certain deductions or credits. Correspondence audits involve the IRS and the taxpayer communicating in writing, with requests for information or clarification sent via mail or electronic means. To address the IRS's concerns, S corporation owners should respond promptly and provide the requested documentation or explanations.

2. Office audits:

Office audits necessitate S corporation owners visiting an IRS office to meet with an IRS agent in person. The IRS agent will review specific aspects of the tax return in greater detail during an office audit and may request additional documentation or clarification. These audits are usually performed for more complex tax issues or when the IRS requests a closer look at the S corporation's financial records. Owners must thoroughly prepare for office audits by gathering all relevant documentation and being ready to address any questions or concerns raised by the IRS agent.

3. Field audits:

The most thorough and intrusive type of IRS audit is the field audit. They entail an IRS agent conducting a thorough examination of the S corporation's financial records and operations at the business premises or another specified location. Field audits are typically reserved for cases involving complex tax issues, significant discrepancies, or suspected fraud. The IRS agent will review all relevant financial records, interview key personnel, and potentially conduct a thorough examination of the business's operations during a field audit. To facilitate the audit process, S corporation owners should seek professional assistance and ensure that all requested documentation and information are readily available.

S-corporation owners must understand the scope and procedures associated with each type of IRS audit. By understanding the various types of audits, owners can better prepare themselves and their financial records, ensuring that they are prepared to respond to any audit inquiries or requests for documentation.

Owners should keep open lines of communication with the IRS agent assigned to their case during an audit, respond promptly to any requests or inquiries, and provide accurate and complete information. Seeking professional assistance from a qualified tax advisor or CPA with audit experience can also help you navigate the audit process and ensure compliance with IRS regulations.

Finally, understanding the various types of IRS audits and their scope enables S corporation owners to plan ahead of time for the audit process. Whether it's a correspondence audit, an office audit, or a field audit, knowing the procedures and requirements allows owners to gather the necessary documentation, address any concerns, and effectively respond to IRS inquiries. S corporation owners can successfully navigate the IRS audit process and achieve a satisfactory resolution if they approach the audit with preparation and cooperation.

12.4 Audit risk reduction strategies based on proper reporting and documentation

This section delves into methods for reducing audit risks through proper reporting and documentation. S corporation owners can improve their compliance efforts and reduce the likelihood of IRS inquiries or audits by implementing these strategies.

1. Accurate reporting:

Accurate reporting is critical for reducing audit risks. Owners of S corporations should make certain that all financial information, including income, expenses, and deductions, is accurately reported on their tax returns. This necessitates a thorough examination and verification of financial records, such as bank statements, invoices, receipts, and other supporting documentation. Owners can reduce the risk of errors or discrepancies attracting IRS attention by double-checking the accuracy of reported information.

2. Financial statement consistency:

Financial statement consistency is critical for minimizing audit risks. S corporation owners should keep financial information consistent across documents such as tax returns, financial statements, and supporting schedules. Inconsistencies or discrepancies in reporting may raise red flags during IRS audits, leading to inquiries or audits. Owners can demonstrate transparency and dependability by ensuring consistency in financial statements, reducing the likelihood of IRS scrutiny.

3. Thorough documentation of deductions and credits:

Proper documentation of deductions and credits is essential for proving claimed tax benefits and reducing audit risks. Owners of S corporations should keep detailed records of all deductible expenses, including receipts, invoices, contracts, and other relevant documentation. They should also keep records of any credits claimed, such as R&D credits or energy-efficient property credits. In the event of an IRS audit, thorough documentation provides evidence and substantiation for deductions and credits, allowing owners to defend their tax positions.

4. Seek professional help:

Using the services of a qualified tax professional, such as a CPA or tax advisor, can help reduce audit risks. These professionals have the knowledge and expertise to ensure accurate reporting, IRS compliance, and proper documentation. They can review the S corporation's financial records, identify potential areas of concern, and advise on best reporting and documentation practices. S corporation owners can address compliance issues proactively and reduce the likelihood of IRS inquiries or audits by working with professionals.

5. Keep informed and up-to-date:

Keeping up with changes in tax laws and regulations is critical for reducing audit risks. S-corporation owners should stay up-to-date on any changes to tax laws that may affect their reporting obligations. Staying current allows owners to make necessary changes to their reporting processes and ensure compliance with the most recent IRS requirements.

Finally, S corporation owners must implement strategies for reducing audit risks through proper reporting and documentation. Owners can reduce the likelihood of IRS inquiries or audits by maintaining accurate reporting, consistency in financial statements, and thorough documentation of deductions and credits. Seeking professional help and staying up-to-date on tax regulations helps strengthen compliance efforts. S corporation owners can improve their overall compliance, reduce audit risks, and maintain a strong financial position by implementing these strategies.

12.5 S corporation audit preparation, including gathering supporting documentation and engaging professional assistance

In this section, we explain how to prepare for an S corporation audit. Adequate preparation is essential for successfully navigating the audit process and dealing with any potential issues that may arise. S corporation owners can improve their chances of a successful audit outcome by following these steps.

1. **Gather supporting documentation:** Obtaining supporting documentation is an important part of audit preparation. S corporation owners should gather and organize all pertinent financial records, such as bank statements, invoices, receipts, contracts, and other supporting documents. These records should accurately reflect the income, expenses, deductions,

credits, and other financial transactions of the company. Owners can substantiate their reported figures and provide evidence to support their tax positions during an audit if they have comprehensive documentation readily available.

2. **Organize financial records:** Keeping financial records organized is critical for a smooth audit process. Owners should keep their records organized and easily accessible. This includes document categorization, maintaining a systematic filing system, and clearly labeling various types of records. A well-organized recordkeeping system allows owners to quickly locate and present the requested information during an audit, demonstrating compliance and easing the audit process.

3. **Engage professional assistance:** During an audit, professional assistance, such as tax advisors or Certified Public Accountants (CPAs), can be beneficial. These experts are knowledgeable about tax regulations and audit procedures, and they can provide valuable guidance and support throughout the process. They can examine the S corporation's financial records, assist in the interpretation of complex tax rules, and advise on the best ways to present the information to the IRS. Their participation can increase trust in the accuracy and validity of the reported figures, increasing the chances of a favorable audit outcome.

4. **Conduct a mock audit:** A mock audit can help S corporation owners identify and address potential weaknesses in their reporting. Owners can identify any areas of concern, such as inconsistent records, missing documentation, or unclear

reporting practices, by simulating an audit process internally or with the assistance of a professional. A mock audit allows owners to address these issues in advance, reducing the likelihood of IRS inquiries or disputes during the actual audit.

5. **Familiarize yourself with audit procedures:** S corporation owners should become acquainted with the IRS audit procedures. Understanding the audit process, the types of inquiries that may arise, and the taxpayer's rights and responsibilities can help owners mentally and emotionally prepare for the audit. Owners can respond confidently and effectively during the audit if they know what to expect, ensuring compliance and minimizing potential disruptions to their business operations.

Finally, thorough preparation is required when facing a S corporation audit. Owners can navigate the audit process more smoothly and confidently by gathering supporting documentation, organizing financial records, engaging professional assistance, conducting a mock audit, and becoming familiar with audit procedures. Adequate planning increases the likelihood of a favorable audit outcome and ensures compliance with IRS regulations.

12.6 Navigating the audit process, responding to IRS inquiries, and dealing with potential problems

We explain how to navigate the audit process, respond to IRS inquiries, and address potential issues that may arise during a S corporation audit in this section. S corporation owners can effectively manage the audit and work toward a favorable resolution if they follow these steps.

1. **Prompt and accurate responses:**

   Throughout the audit process, prompt and accurate responses to IRS inquiries are critical. Owners should carefully review any IRS inquiries or requests for information and respond in a comprehensive and accurate manner within the timeframe specified. It is crucial to make sure that all information is correct, backed up by evidence, and matches the S corporation's financial records. Owners demonstrate their cooperation and commitment to compliance by responding in a timely and accurate manner, which can positively influence the audit's outcome.

2. **Role of documentation:**

   Documentation plays an important role in supporting claims and defending positions taken on the S corporation's tax returns. Owners should be prepared to provide relevant and well-organized documentation to substantiate the reported figures and transactions during an audit. Invoices, receipts, contracts, bank statements, and any other records that validate the accuracy of the reported financial information may be included. Thorough documentation enhances the credibility of the S corporation's tax positions and can aid in the resolution of any discrepancies or concerns raised by the IRS.

3. **Resolving disagreements or disputes:**

During the audit process, disagreements or disputes may arise between the S corporation and the IRS. Owners must understand their rights and options for resolving such issues. Negotiation and communication with the IRS can frequently result in a resolution. If an agreement cannot be reached, owners can take additional steps, such as appealing the audit findings through the IRS appeals process or seeking professional legal assistance. Understanding the various dispute resolution options enables owners to protect their interests and ensure a fair resolution.

4. **Maintain professionalism and cooperation:**

It is critical to maintain professionalism and a cooperative attitude when dealing with IRS representatives throughout the audit process. Responding to inquiries, providing requested documentation, and participating in meetings or discussions with the IRS should all be done with courtesy and cooperation. Professionalism and cooperation can aid in establishing a positive rapport with the IRS and facilitating a more amicable and efficient audit resolution.

5. **Seek professional help if necessary:**

If owners face complex or difficult issues during the audit, it may be beneficial to seek professional help from tax advisors, CPAs, or tax attorneys. These experts can provide expert advice, interpret complex tax laws, and represent the interests of the S corporation during the audit process. Their knowledge and experience can assist in navigating potential challenges and ensuring that the rights of the S corporation are protected throughout the audit.

To summarize, navigating the audit process necessitates owners responding to IRS inquiries promptly and accurately, relying on documentation to support claims, and dealing with potential issues in a proactive and cooperative manner. Owners can improve their chances of a favorable resolution by approaching the audit process diligently and seeking professional assistance when necessary.

12.7 Options for appeals and dispute resolution in the event of an unfavorable audit outcome

This section discusses the appeals and dispute resolution options available to S corporation owners who receive a negative audit result. Understanding these options is critical for owners seeking to protect their rights and reach fair resolutions with the IRS.

1. **Filing an appeal:**

   If a business owner disagrees with the audit findings, he or she may file an appeal with the IRS. The appeals process allows the S corporation to present additional evidence, arguments, or clarifications to support its position. When an appeal is filed, it triggers a separate review by an independent appeals officer, who can reconsider the audit findings and propose a resolution. Owners who participate in the appeals process can present their case in a more formal and structured manner and seek a fair outcome.

2. **Requesting a conference:**

   Before filing an appeal, owners can request a conference with the IRS to discuss the audit findings and seek a resolution. A conference allows for an open dialogue between the owner and the IRS representative in order to address any concerns or disagreements. Owners can present their arguments, provide additional documentation, and negotiate potential settlements during the conference. Requesting a conference shows a willingness to resolve the issues amicably and can lead to a mutually acceptable resolution without the need for formal appeals or litigation.

3. **Alternative dispute resolution methods:**

   In addition to appeals and conferences, the IRS provides alternative dispute resolution (ADR) methods to help taxpayers and the IRS resolve disagreements. ADR methods such as mediation and arbitration offer a less formal and more collaborative approach to dispute resolution. These methods entail the use of a neutral third party to facilitate discussions and assist the parties in reaching a resolution. For owners who prefer a more informal and expedited resolution process, ADR may be a viable option.

4. **Seeking professional help:**

   Navigating the appeals and dispute resolution processes can be difficult, so owners may benefit from seeking professional help from tax advisors, CPAs, or tax attorneys. These experts are well-versed in tax laws and the appeals process, and they can offer valuable advice and representation during negotiations or proceedings. Professional help can help the owner present a strong case, protect their rights, and achieve a favorable resolution.

S corporation owners can assert their rights and seek fair resolutions with the IRS if they understand the available appeals and dispute resolution options. Owners can address unfavorable audit outcomes and work toward a resolution that is in their best interests by filing an appeal, requesting a conference, or exploring alternative dispute resolution methods. Seeking professional help when necessary can help strengthen their position and increase the chances of a successful resolution.

12.8 Preventive measures to reduce the possibility of future audits and improve compliance

This section discusses proactive steps that S corporation owners can take to reduce the likelihood of future audits and improve overall compliance. Owners can reduce audit risks and maintain a strong compliance posture by implementing these strategies.

1. **Implementing internal controls:**

   Establishing strong internal controls within the S corporation is critical for keeping accurate financial records and adhering to tax regulations. Financial transactions, record-keeping, and reporting are all governed by internal controls, which include procedures and policies. Owners can reduce the risk of errors, inconsistencies, or fraudulent activities that may trigger an audit by implementing effective internal controls. Segregation of duties, regular reconciliations, and periodic reviews of financial records are examples of controls.

2. **Conducting periodic reviews:**

Reviewing financial records, tax returns, and other relevant documents on a regular basis can assist in identifying potential discrepancies or errors that may attract IRS scrutiny. Owners can detect and correct any inaccuracies or inconsistencies by conducting periodic reviews. It is also an opportunity to ensure that all required documentation is kept up-to-date and readily available in the event of an audit. Owners can address any compliance issues and make necessary corrections before they escalate into audit triggers by conducting internal reviews.

3. **Keeping up with tax law changes:**

   Tax laws and regulations are constantly changing and being updated. Maintaining compliance with current tax requirements requires staying informed about these changes. Owners should stay current on tax laws and regulations that apply to S corporations and make any necessary changes to their reporting and compliance practices. Seeking advice from tax professionals, attending seminars or workshops, and using reliable sources for tax law updates are all examples of this. Being up-to-date on the latest developments ensures that owners are in compliance with current regulations and reduces the risk of non-compliance.

4. **Seeking professional assistance:**

   Seeking advice from tax advisors, CPAs, or tax attorneys can help ensure compliance and reduce audit risks. These professionals are knowledgeable about tax laws and regulations and can provide valuable insights and advice tailored to the S corporation's specific needs. They can aid in the interpretation of complex tax provisions, the resolution of compliance issues, and the implementation of effective strategies to improve overall compliance. Engaging professional assistance can assist owners in navigating the complex tax landscape and ensuring compliance with regulations.

S corporation owners can reduce the likelihood of future audits and improve overall compliance by implementing internal controls, conducting periodic reviews, staying up-to-date on tax law changes, and seeking professional assistance as needed. These proactive measures not only reduce audit risks, but also contribute to the S corporation's tax affairs being managed efficiently and accurately. Owners can focus on their core business activities with confidence and peace of mind if they maintain a strong compliance posture.

Conclusion

S corporation owners can protect their businesses, avoid penalties, and maintain financial stability by proactively addressing IRS compliance requirements and implementing strategies to mitigate audit risks. This chapter has covered the various aspects of S corporation audits, IRS compliance requirements, and the steps owners can take to successfully navigate the audit process.

Understanding the triggers and selection criteria for S corporation audits enables owners to identify and address potential areas of concern. Keeping accurate and well-organized financial records provides the documentation required to support IRS compliance and effectively respond to inquiries. Evaluating various types of audits assists owners in preparing for the unique requirements and expectations of each. Audit risk reduction strategies, such as proper reporting and documentation, reduce the likelihood of IRS inquiries and improve overall compliance.

Preparing for an S corporation audit entails gathering supporting documentation and enlisting professional help to ensure that owners can effectively present their case and address any potential issues that may arise. Navigating the audit process, responding to IRS inquiries, and dealing with potential issues all necessitate timely and accurate responses, as well as the use of proper documentation to support claims. Owners have access to appeals and dispute resolution options in the event of an unfavorable audit outcome to protect their rights and seek fair resolutions.

Taking proactive measures to reduce the likelihood of future audits and improve compliance is also critical. Internal controls, periodic reviews, staying up-to-date on tax law changes, and seeking professional assistance are all valuable steps that owners can take to maintain a strong compliance posture.

S corporation owners can establish a culture of compliance, minimize audit risks, and maintain the financial stability of their businesses by following these guidelines and incorporating these strategies into their business practices. Compliance with IRS regulations not only protects the business, but it also instills confidence in stakeholders and strengthens the S corporation's overall reputation.

S corporation owners can navigate the complex tax landscape with confidence and peace of mind by recognizing the importance of IRS compliance and implementing proactive measures. This allows them to focus on their core business activities and achieve their long-term goals.

Chapter 13: S Corporation Tax Planning for Changing Circumstances

Introduction

As small businesses evolve and adapt to changing circumstances, it becomes increasingly important to adjust tax strategies and seize new opportunities. This chapter examines the dynamic nature of S corporation tax planning and offers advice on how to adapt tax strategies to changing business conditions, regulatory changes, and economic shifts.

Key topics covered in this chapter include:

1. Recognizing common triggers for changes in tax planning strategies for S corporations.
2. Adjusting compensation structures and distributions in response to business growth or downturns.
3. Assessing the impact of economic factors, such as inflation or interest rate changes, on tax planning.
4. Strategies for navigating changes in tax laws, regulations, and provisions.
5. Adapting retirement planning strategies as business owners near retirement or experience financial shifts.
6. Evaluating the tax consequences of significant business transactions, such as mergers, acquisitions, or expansions.
7. Maximizing tax benefits through strategic timing of business expenditures and investments.
8. Regularly reviewing and updating tax planning strategies to ensure ongoing compliance and optimization.

By embracing flexibility and regularly reassessing tax planning strategies, S corporation owners can adapt to changing circumstances, minimize tax liabilities, and maintain financial resilience.

13.1 Recognizing common triggers for changes in S corporation tax planning strategies

This section focuses on identifying common triggers that may necessitate changes in S corporation tax planning strategies. S corporation owners must be aware of these triggers in order to proactively evaluate and modify their tax planning strategies. Owners can ensure that their tax strategies align with their changing business needs by keeping an eye on the following factors:

1. **Business expansion:** As a company expands and grows, it may be necessary to rethink tax planning strategies. Increased revenues, higher operating expenses, and additional employees can all have an impact on a S corporation's tax implications. Tax planning adjustments may be necessary to maximize deductions, credits, and other tax benefits available to growing businesses.

2. **Changes in ownership:** Changes in ownership, such as the addition or departure of shareholders, can necessitate a review of tax planning strategies. Changes in ownership structure may necessitate changes in profit allocation, distributions, or even entity classification. It is critical to align tax planning strategies with the new ownership dynamics.

3. **Industry trends and regulatory changes:** Industry trends and regulatory changes can have a significant impact on tax planning strategies. For example, new tax breaks, credits, or

deductions tailored to specific industries may emerge, providing opportunities for tax planning. Regulatory changes, on the other hand, may limit previously available tax benefits. It is critical to stay informed about industry-specific tax considerations in order to adjust tax planning strategies accordingly.

4. **Shifts in tax legislation:** Tax laws change frequently, and changes in tax legislation can have a significant impact on S corporation tax planning. New tax provisions, changes to existing tax rates, or changes to deductions and credits can all have an impact on the overall tax landscape. Owners of S corporations should stay up to date on tax law changes and assess their impact on current tax planning strategies.

S corporation owners can proactively evaluate and modify their approaches by recognizing these common triggers for changes in tax planning strategies. This adaptability ensures that tax planning remains in line with the changing needs of the business, maximizing tax benefits while minimizing potential risks or liabilities.

13.2 Changing compensation structures and distributions to reflect business growth or decline

This section emphasizes the importance of tailoring compensation structures and distributions to the specific circumstances of business growth or decline. It is critical to optimize the mix of salary and distributions in order to minimize tax liabilities and maximize tax savings. When making changes, S corporation owners should consider the following strategies:

1. **Setting reasonable compensation:** S corporation owners must ensure that they are compensated fairly for the services they provide to the company. The amount that would normally be paid to an individual in a comparable role in a comparable business is referred to as reasonable compensation. Setting a reasonable salary helps to avoid potential IRS scrutiny and ensures tax compliance.

2. **Evaluating profit distributions:** It is critical to evaluate profit distributions as the business grows or declines. During periods of expansion, it may be appropriate to increase profit distributions in order to reward shareholders and provide a reasonable return on investment. In contrast, during downturns, reducing or temporarily suspending distributions may be necessary to preserve cash flow and support the financial stability of the business.

3. **Adapting to changing financial circumstances:** Businesses go through various financial cycles, and compensation structures and distributions must be adjusted accordingly. During times of expansion, owners may consider reinvesting profits back into the business to fund expansion, R&D, or other strategic initiatives. During economic downturns or times of financial constraint, however, owners may need to prioritize maintaining cash reserves and reducing distributions to ensure the business's viability.

S corporation owners can align their tax planning strategies with the changing dynamics of their business by reviewing and adjusting compensation structures and distributions on a regular basis. This approach enables them to maximize tax savings, effectively manage cash flow, and support the company's long-term financial health. It is critical to seek the advice of tax professionals or financial advisors to ensure that any changes comply with tax laws and regulations.

13.3 Evaluating the impact of economic factors on tax planning, such as inflation or interest rate changes

This section delves into the evaluation of economic factors and their impact on S corporation tax planning. Economic changes, such as inflation or interest rate fluctuations, can have a significant impact on tax strategies. To navigate these factors and optimize their tax planning, S corporation owners should consider the following strategies:

1. **Inflation mitigation:** Over time, inflation can erode the purchasing power of money, affecting the financial landscape for S corporations. Owners can consider strategies such as accelerated depreciation methods, cost-of-living adjustments in employee compensation, and utilizing tax provisions that offer inflationary safeguards to mitigate the impact of inflation on tax planning. Furthermore, investing in assets that appreciate with inflation can help offset the effects of rising prices on the overall financial health of the business.

2. **Managing interest rate fluctuations:** Interest rate fluctuations can have an impact on borrowing costs, investments, and debt management strategies. Owners of S corporations should closely monitor interest rate trends and assess the implications for their tax planning. For example,

during low-interest rate periods, owners may consider refinancing existing debt to benefit from lower interest expenses. During periods of high interest rates, on the other hand, they may prioritize minimizing interest payments and exploring alternative financing options.

3. **Utilizing tax provisions affected by economic changes:** Economic factors can have an impact on specific tax provisions or incentives. Owners of S corporations should stay up-to-date on changes in tax laws and regulations related to economic conditions. During periods of economic stimulus, for example, certain tax credits or deductions may be available to encourage investment, research and development, or job creation. Owners can optimize their tax positions by understanding these provisions and their potential benefits.

S corporation owners can adapt their strategies and make informed decisions by assessing the impact of economic factors on tax planning. It is critical to keep up with economic trends, consult with tax professionals or financial advisors, and assess the specific implications for the business. This proactive approach ensures that tax planning is in line with current economic conditions and that tax benefits for the S corporation are maximized.

13.4 Strategies for navigating changes in tax laws, regulations, and provisions

In this section, we look at how to navigate changes in tax laws, regulations, and provisions that may affect S corporations. Maintaining compliance and optimizing tax planning require staying up-to-date on tax updates and understanding the implications of new rules. The following strategies can assist S corporation owners in effectively navigating these changes:

1. **Stay informed:** It is critical to keep up to date on changes in tax laws, regulations, and provisions that affect S corporations. Review tax authority updates, such as the Internal Revenue Service (IRS), on a regular basis, and consult reputable sources, such as tax publications or professional tax organizations. By staying informed, business owners can anticipate changes that may affect their tax planning strategies.

2. **Work with tax professionals:** Engage the services of experienced tax professionals, such as tax advisors or certified public accountants (CPAs), to provide valuable guidance when navigating changes in tax laws. These professionals are well-versed in tax regulations and can assist in the interpretation of new rules, assessing their impact on the business, and recommending appropriate adjustments to tax planning strategies. Their knowledge can help ensure compliance and identify tax-saving opportunities.

3. **Use available resources:** There are numerous resources available to help S corporation owners understand and implement changes in tax laws and regulations. Tax publications, online guides, seminars, and workshops offered by tax authorities or professional organizations are examples of these resources. Using these resources can help to improve understanding, clarify any uncertainties, and provide insights

into how to adapt tax planning strategies to meet new requirements.

4. **Conduct regular tax planning reviews:** Because tax laws and provisions are constantly changing, it is critical to conduct regular reviews of tax planning strategies. Examine existing plans for alignment with the current tax landscape. Determine which areas may require adjustments or optimization as a result of the new rules. S corporation owners can identify potential risks, seize tax-saving opportunities, and stay in compliance with the latest tax laws by conducting proactive reviews.

5. **Create a proactive compliance culture:** Creating a compliance culture within the S corporation entails establishing internal processes and procedures to monitor and ensure compliance with tax laws and regulations. This includes proper tax documentation, record-keeping, and internal controls. S corporation owners can reduce the risk of noncompliance and effectively respond to changes in tax laws and regulations by establishing a proactive compliance culture.

Keeping up with changes in tax laws, regulations, and provisions necessitates a proactive approach. S corporation owners can effectively navigate these changes by staying informed, working with tax professionals, utilizing available resources, conducting regular reviews, and fostering a culture of compliance. This enables them to optimize their tax planning strategies, maximize tax savings, and stay in compliance with ever-changing tax requirements.

13.5 Changing retirement planning strategies as business owners approach retirement or face financial changes

This section emphasizes the importance of S corporation owners adapting retirement planning strategies as they approach retirement or face financial changes. It investigates various options for maximizing tax benefits and ensuring a secure financial future. The following key points emphasize the importance of modifying retirement planning strategies:

1. **Qualified retirement plans:** S corporation owners may wish to consider qualified retirement plans such as 401(k) plans, SEP IRAs (Simplified Employee Pension Individual Retirement Accounts), or SIMPLE IRAs (Savings Incentive Match Plan for Employees Individual Retirement Accounts). These plans provide tax benefits by allowing owners to contribute pre-tax income while potentially receiving employer matching contributions. Including qualified retirement plans in retirement planning strategies can help owners accumulate savings while enjoying tax benefits.

2. **Individual Retirement Accounts (IRAs):** IRAs are another way to save for retirement. Depending on their eligibility and tax objectives, S corporation owners can contribute to traditional or Roth IRAs. Traditional IRAs may provide tax breaks on contributions, whereas Roth IRAs allow for tax-free withdrawals in retirement. Evaluating and adapting retirement planning strategies to include IRAs can increase tax benefits while also providing flexibility in retirement income planning.

3. **Succession planning:** As business owners approach retirement age, succession planning becomes increasingly important. This entails identifying and training a successor to take over the company. Including succession planning in retirement planning strategies ensures a smooth transition of the business while accounting for tax implications. Proper succession planning can help reduce tax burdens and ensure business continuity for future generations.

4. **Tax optimization:** When adapting retirement planning strategies, the tax implications of various retirement vehicles and distribution strategies must be considered. Owners can look into Roth conversions, which involve transferring funds from traditional retirement accounts to Roth accounts, potentially resulting in tax-free withdrawals in retirement. Owners can maximize their retirement savings and reduce their tax liabilities by strategically assessing tax optimization opportunities.

5. **Financial changes and adjustments:** Changes in business profitability or personal financial circumstances may necessitate adjustments to retirement planning strategies. Changing contributions, investment allocations, or retirement income projections in response to changing financial conditions ensures that retirement goals remain realistic and reachable. To align retirement planning strategies with changing circumstances, regular assessments and adjustments are required.

S-corporation owners can maximize tax benefits and secure their financial future by implementing retirement planning strategies. Qualified retirement plans, IRAs, succession planning, and tax optimization strategies are all important components of ensuring a comfortable retirement. Owners can align their retirement planning with changing financial circumstances and tax objectives with regular reviews and adjustments, providing peace of mind and financial stability during their retirement years.

13.6 Assessing the tax implications of major business transactions such as mergers, acquisitions, or expansions

This section delves into the tax implications of major business transactions such as mergers, acquisitions, and expansions. These transactions can have significant implications for S corporations' tax positions, and it is critical for owners to evaluate and plan for the tax consequences. During these transformative events, the following key considerations can assist S corporation owners in navigating the tax landscape:

1. **Basis adjustments:** It is critical to assess the basis of acquired assets or stock when engaging in a significant business transaction, such as a merger or acquisition. Understanding the basis adjustments can assist in determining the tax consequences and potential tax savings. Accounting for basis adjustments correctly ensures accurate reporting and compliance with tax laws.

2. **Transaction structures:** The business transaction structure chosen can have varying tax implications. Each structure has its own tax considerations, whether it is a stock purchase, an

asset purchase, or a merger. Evaluating the tax implications of various transaction structures can assist S corporation owners in making informed decisions that are in line with their tax objectives and minimize tax liabilities.

3. **Opportunities for tax planning:** Significant business transactions provide opportunities for tax planning. Owners may be able to achieve tax efficiencies by strategically structuring the transaction, such as utilizing net operating losses, maximizing depreciation deductions, or optimizing the treatment of goodwill. Identifying and incorporating these opportunities into the transaction planning process can result in significant tax savings.

4. **Minimizing tax liabilities:** Owners should investigate strategies to reduce tax liabilities during major business transactions. This could include properly allocating the purchase price, determining the tax treatment of contingent payments, or taking advantage of available tax provisions or incentives. Using the services of tax professionals and advisors who specialize in mergers, acquisitions, or expansions can assist in identifying opportunities to reduce tax liabilities and optimize the overall tax position.

5. **Compliance with tax laws:** It is critical to ensure that all applicable tax laws and regulations are followed during major business transactions. To avoid potential tax penalties and ensure the accuracy of tax filings, owners should carefully navigate tax provisions related to change in control, anti-abuse rules, or deduction limitations.

S corporation owners can make informed decisions and plan for tax implications by evaluating the tax consequences of significant business transactions. Owners can optimize their tax position and achieve their business objectives by considering factors such as basis adjustments, transaction structures, tax planning opportunities, minimizing tax liabilities, and compliance with tax laws. Seeking the advice of tax professionals and advisors with experience in business transactions can provide valuable insights and ensure tax compliance.

13.7 Increasing tax benefits by strategically timing business expenditures and investments

This section focuses on the importance of strategic timing in business expenditures and investments for S corporations. Timing these activities correctly can have a significant impact on maximizing tax benefits and optimizing the overall tax position. The following crucial considerations highlight the significance of strategic timing decisions:

1. **Depreciation deductions:** The timing of business expenditures, particularly those related to asset acquisition, can have an impact on the depreciation deductions available to S corporations. Owners can maximize depreciation deductions, such as bonus depreciation and Section 179 expensing, by strategically planning the timing of asset purchases. This can result in immediate tax savings as well as improved cash flow.

2. **Capital gains treatment:** The timing of the sale or disposition of business assets can affect how capital gains are taxed. Owners can strategically plan to take advantage of lower capital gains tax rates by realizing capital gains during favorable tax periods. Deferring the sale of assets, on the other hand, can be advantageous in certain circumstances, such as when the business is subject to higher tax rates or when there are plans for future tax planning opportunities.

3. **Tax credits:** Some business expenditures and investments, such as R&D credits or renewable energy incentives, may be eligible for tax credits. Strategic timing of these activities can ensure that S corporations meet the required criteria and maximize their tax credit eligibility. Owners can reduce their overall tax liability and increase cash flow by aligning these expenditures with the appropriate tax credit provisions.

4. **Net operating losses:** The timing of business expenditures and investments can affect the use of net operating losses (NOLs). NOLs can be carried forward or backward in order to offset future or past taxable income. Owners can maximize the use of NOLs and potentially generate tax refunds or reduce future tax liabilities by strategically timing expenditures and investments.

5. **Changing tax laws and provisions:** It is critical to stay informed about changing tax laws and provisions when making strategic timing decisions. Monitoring legislative updates, such as tax rate changes or expiring tax incentives, enables business owners to plan and execute their

expenditures and investments to maximize available tax benefits. Reviewing tax law changes on a regular basis ensures that S corporations remain compliant and can adjust their timing strategies accordingly.

S corporation owners can strategically plan their business expenditures and investments to maximize tax benefits by understanding the tax implications of timing decisions. Depreciation deductions, capital gains treatment, tax credit eligibility, NOL utilization, and awareness of changing tax laws all contribute to optimizing the timing of these activities. Consultation with tax professionals or advisors can provide useful insights and assist owners in making well-informed decisions that align with their tax objectives and improve their overall tax position.

13.8 Reviewing and updating tax planning strategies on a regular basis to ensure ongoing compliance and optimization

In this section, we emphasize the importance of reviewing and updating tax planning strategies for S corporations on a regular basis. Because tax laws are dynamic and business conditions change, ongoing assessments are required to ensure compliance and optimization. The following key points emphasize the importance of regular reviews:

1. **Compliance with tax laws:** Regular audits assist S corporations in remaining in compliance with ever-changing tax laws and regulations. Tax laws are frequently updated, and new provisions that affect the tax landscape may be introduced. Owners can ensure ongoing compliance and avoid

potential penalties or audit risks by reviewing tax planning strategies on a regular basis.

2. **Staying up to date on tax law changes:** Staying up to date on tax law changes is critical for effective tax planning. S corporation owners can stay informed about new legislation, regulations, or court decisions that may affect their tax positions by conducting regular reviews. Owners who stay current can proactively adapt their strategies to capitalize on new opportunities or mitigate potential challenges posed by tax law changes.

3. **Maximizing tax benefits:** Regular reviews allow you to optimize your tax planning strategies and maximize your tax benefits. Over time, business circumstances, financial goals, and tax objectives may change. Owners can identify opportunities to reduce tax liabilities, take advantage of available tax incentives, and improve overall tax efficiency by conducting regular assessments.

4. **Collaboration with tax professionals:** Effective tax planning requires collaboration with tax professionals or advisors. Regular reviews enable ongoing communication with tax professionals, providing expert insights and guidance. These experts can provide valuable insight, assist in the interpretation of complex tax regulations, and make strategic recommendations tailored to the specific needs of S corporations. Their knowledge ensures that tax planning strategies remain strong and up-to-date with the latest best practices.

5. **Changing business circumstances and objectives:** Business circumstances and objectives can change over time. Regular reviews allow S corporation owners to determine whether their current tax planning strategies align with their changing business needs. They provide an opportunity to assess whether current strategies are still effective or if changes are needed to optimize tax positions and support the business's long-term growth, profitability, or other goals.

S corporation owners can ensure ongoing compliance with tax laws, stay informed about changes, and engage with tax professionals for optimization by conducting regular reviews of tax planning strategies. This proactive approach contributes to the integrity of tax planning strategies, the maximization of tax benefits, and the adaptation to the changing needs of the business. Regular reviews provide an invaluable opportunity to fine-tune strategies and ensure that S corporations remain tax-efficient.

Conclusion

The key to successful S corporation tax planning is to embrace flexibility and reassess strategies on a regular basis. S corporation owners can effectively adapt to changing circumstances, reduce tax liabilities, and maintain financial resilience by doing so. The following points summarize the significance of adaptability and regular reevaluation:

1. **Adapting to changing circumstances:** Because business environments are dynamic, S corporations' tax planning

strategies must be adjusted accordingly. Owners can proactively evaluate and modify their approaches to maintain tax efficiency by recognizing common triggers for strategy changes, such as business growth, regulatory changes, or ownership changes.

2. **Maximizing tax benefits:** Tax benefits can be maximized by adjusting compensation structures, distributions, and retirement planning strategies based on business growth or downturns. Adapting retirement planning strategies such as qualified retirement plans, IRAs, and succession planning ensures tax efficiency and financial security.

3. **Navigating economic factors:** Economic factors such as inflation or changes in interest rates can have a significant impact on tax planning. S corporation owners can make informed decisions and optimize their tax positions by assessing their impact and implementing strategies to mitigate their effects.

4. **Staying informed and compliant:** Tax laws, regulations, and provisions are constantly changing, necessitating constant vigilance. Reviewing and updating tax planning strategies on a regular basis ensures ongoing compliance and takes advantage of new opportunities. Owners can effectively navigate changes by working with tax professionals and utilizing available resources.

5. **Strategic timing and optimization:** Using provisions such as depreciation deductions, capital gains treatment, or eligibility

for tax credits, strategic timing of business expenditures and investments can maximize tax benefits. Reevaluating tax planning strategies on a regular basis assists owners in identifying optimal timing opportunities and increasing tax savings.

S corporation owners can adapt to changing circumstances, minimize tax liabilities, and maintain financial resilience by embracing flexibility and conducting regular reassessments. Staying informed and engaging with tax professionals are essential for ensuring tax efficiency and optimizing financial outcomes. S corporation owners can position their businesses for long-term success by taking a proactive and adaptive approach to tax planning.

Chapter 14: S Corporation State and Local Tax Considerations

Introduction

While federal taxes are frequently highlighted, it is critical for S corporation owners to understand the complexities of state and local taxes as well. This chapter delves into the implications and considerations of state and local taxation for S corporations, offering valuable insights to help owners minimize tax burdens and ensure compliance with jurisdiction-specific requirements.

Key topics covered in this chapter include:

1. Understanding the fundamentals of state and local taxation and its application to S corporations.
2. Navigating the complexities of state income tax laws and calculating S corporation tax liabilities on a state-by-state basis.
3. Considerations for S corporations in multiple states, including nexus and apportionment rules.
4. Legal and permissible strategies for reducing state and local tax burdens.
5. Compliance and reporting requirements for S corporations operating in multiple jurisdictions.
6. Considering the effect of state and local tax breaks and credits on S corporation tax planning.
7. Addressing the challenges and common pitfalls of state and local tax compliance.
8. Case studies demonstrating the application of state and local tax considerations in the taxation of S corporations.

S corporation owners can optimize their tax position, reduce compliance risks, and effectively manage their overall tax obligations by proactively addressing state and local tax considerations.

14.1 Understanding the fundamentals of state and local taxation and its application to S corporations

In this section, we provide a thorough overview of the fundamentals of state and local taxation, emphasizing their importance for S corporations. We investigate the various types of taxes levied at the state and local levels, as well as the reasons why S corporation owners must navigate these complexities.

We begin by discussing state and local taxation, which refers to taxes imposed by individual states as well as counties, cities, and other local jurisdictions. We go over how these taxes differ from federal taxes, as well as the different legal frameworks that govern them.

After that, we'll examine the various types of taxes that state and local governments frequently impose. Income taxes, sales taxes, property taxes, payroll taxes, and various fees and assessments are examples. We explain the purpose and characteristics of each tax type, as well as the implications for S corporations.

Understanding state and local taxation is important for S corporation owners because it has a direct impact on their businesses. State and local taxes, unlike federal taxes, are frequently jurisdiction-specific, meaning they differ from one location to the next. S corporations must follow the tax laws, regulations, and compliance requirements of each state and local jurisdiction.

Furthermore, state and local taxes can have a significant impact on the financial obligations and overall tax liabilities of S corporation owners. S corporation owners can make informed decisions about their business operations, tax planning strategies, and compliance responsibilities if they understand the fundamentals of state and local taxation.

S corporation owners can accurately assess their tax liabilities, take advantage of available deductions and credits, and ensure compliance with jurisdiction-specific requirements by navigating the complexities of state and local taxation. It also enables them to manage their tax obligations effectively, reduce tax burdens, and allocate resources in a way that supports their long-term financial goals.

To summarize, S corporation owners must understand the fundamentals of state and local taxation. Owners can navigate the complexities of state and local taxation more effectively and make informed decisions that optimize their tax positions by understanding the various types of taxes imposed at the state and local levels and the relevance of these taxes to their businesses.

14.2 Navigating the complexities of state income tax laws and calculating state S corporation tax liabilities

This section delves into the complexities of state income tax laws and their implications for S corporations. We look at the factors that influence S corporation tax liabilities at the state level, such as apportionment, sourcing rules, and state-specific deductions and credits.

State income tax laws are critical in determining the tax liabilities of S corporations that operate within a specific state. These statutes set forth the rules and regulations that govern how income is calculated, allocated, and taxed at the state level.

One crucial concept to grasp is apportionment, which determines how much of a S corporation's income is taxable in each state. Apportionment formulas differ by state, but they typically consider factors such as the percentage of sales, property, and payroll attributable to that state. S corporations can allocate their income across different states where they have a presence or conduct business by using these formulas.

The sourcing rules also have an impact on S corporations' state income tax liabilities. These regulations govern how specific types of income, such as sales of goods or services, are allocated to specific states. Understanding the complexities of these rules is critical for correctly reporting income and adhering to state tax regulations.

Furthermore, states may provide specific deductions or credits that can reduce the tax liability of a S corporation. These deductions and credits can vary greatly by state and may be based on factors such as job creation, investment in specific industries, or R&D activities. Knowing about these state-specific provisions enables S corporation owners to optimize their tax positions and potentially lower their state income tax burdens.

Navigating the complexities of state income tax laws necessitates a thorough understanding of each state's specific regulations where an S corporation operates. Owners of S corporations should become acquainted with the relevant state statutes, administrative rules, and guidance provided by state tax authorities. To ensure compliance and maximize tax benefits, it is also advisable to seek professional assistance from tax advisors or CPAs with expertise in state taxation.

S corporation owners can accurately determine their state tax liabilities by effectively navigating the nuances of state income tax laws. Understanding apportionment, sourcing rules, and state-specific deductions or credits allows business owners to comply with state tax regulations, reduce tax burdens, and optimize their overall tax positions.

14.3 Considerations for S corporations in multiple states, including nexus and apportionment rules

Operating as an S corporation in multiple states adds complexity due to different nexus and apportionment rules. This section delves into the concept of nexus and its implications for S corporations, as well as the significance of understanding apportionment rules that distribute income across multiple jurisdictions.

Nexus refers to the minimum connection or presence required for a corporation to be subject to the tax laws of that state. Having a physical presence in a state, conducting business transactions, or employing personnel within the state's borders are all common ways to establish a nexus. Each state has its own set of rules and thresholds for determining nexus, which may include things like sales volume, transaction volume, or the presence of employees or property.

For S corporations that operate in multiple states, determining nexus is critical because it determines which states require them to file tax returns and pay state taxes. Understanding each state's nexus requirements is critical for ensuring compliance with state tax laws and avoiding potential penalties or audits.

When allocating income across multiple jurisdictions for tax purposes, apportionment rules come into play. These rules determine how much of a S corporation's income is attributed to each state in which it operates. Sales, property, and payroll are common apportionment factors used to determine the percentage of income allocated to each state.

Apportionment rules can differ greatly between states, resulting in complex calculations and potentially affecting a S corporation's tax liabilities in each jurisdiction. S corporation owners must understand the apportionment rules of each state in which they have a nexus because accurate calculations are required for determining tax obligations and filing accurate tax returns.

Navigating multistate issues necessitates a thorough understanding of the nexus and apportionment rules in each jurisdiction in which a S corporation operates. It is critical to stay up-to-date on changes in state tax laws and regulations that may have an impact on nexus or apportionment requirements. Consultation with tax professionals who specialize in multistate taxation can provide valuable guidance and assist in ensuring compliance with state tax laws.

S corporation owners can navigate the complexities of operating in multiple states by effectively managing nexus and understanding apportionment rules. Owners can fulfill their tax obligations in each jurisdiction while minimizing the risk of penalties or audits by complying with nexus requirements and performing accurate apportionment calculations.

14.4 Legal and permissible strategies for reducing state and local tax burdens

Reduced state and local tax burdens necessitate careful and strategic planning. In this section, we provide valuable insights into legal and permissible strategies that S corporation owners can use to reduce their tax liabilities in state and local jurisdictions. Owners can optimize their tax positions and maximize tax savings by implementing these strategies.

Taking advantage of available tax credits and incentives provided by state and local governments is an effective strategy. These credits and incentives are intended to encourage specific actions or investments that benefit the local economy. Credits for job creation, R&D, renewable energy projects, or investment in economically distressed areas are some examples. S-corporation owners can significantly reduce their tax burdens while contributing to economic growth by identifying and leveraging these opportunities.

Tax planning techniques are critical to reducing state and local tax burdens. These methods entail making strategic decisions about income recognition, expense timing, and deductions. Owners, for example, can time certain income and expenses to maximize tax benefits. They can potentially reduce their taxable income within a specific state or local jurisdiction by deferring income or accelerating deductible expenses.

Another factor to consider is entity structure. S corporations may consider the benefits of forming subsidiary entities or utilizing pass-through structures that are advantageous in terms of state and local taxes. This could include establishing separate entities to operate in different jurisdictions as well as taking advantage of more favorable tax rates or exemptions available in specific locations. A thorough examination of entity structuring options can result in substantial tax savings while remaining in compliance with applicable laws and regulations.

It is critical to remember that any strategy used to reduce state and local tax burdens must be legal and permissible under the applicable tax laws. It is critical to work with knowledgeable tax professionals to ensure compliance and effectively navigate the complex landscape of state and local tax planning.

S corporation owners can reduce their state and local tax burdens within the bounds of the law by implementing these strategies. Using tax credits, incentives, tax planning techniques, and appropriate entity structuring to optimize tax positions allows owners to achieve significant tax savings while remaining in compliance with state and local tax laws and regulations.

14.5 Compliance and reporting requirements for S corporations operating in multiple jurisdictions

Operating an S corporation in multiple jurisdictions imposes unique compliance and reporting obligations. This section outlines these obligations and emphasizes their significance for S corporations. Understanding and meeting these requirements is critical for avoiding penalties, staying in compliance, and running the business smoothly.

When operating in multiple jurisdictions, S corporations must follow the regulations and guidelines of each state and local tax authority. This includes registering with the relevant tax authorities, obtaining the necessary licenses and permits, and meeting tax filing and payment deadlines.

Filing state income tax returns in each jurisdiction where the S corporation has a tax presence or nexus is a key compliance requirement. This typically entails reporting the corporation's income, deductions, and jurisdiction-specific apportionment factors. Furthermore, some states may require separate reporting for franchise taxes, sales taxes, and other state-specific taxes.

Another critical aspect for S corporations selling taxable goods or services is sales tax compliance. Each jurisdiction may have its own set of rules and reporting requirements for sales taxes. S corporations must collect, report, and remit sales taxes in accordance with the rules of each jurisdiction in which they have a sales tax obligation.

It's critical to keep up with changes in tax laws and regulations in each jurisdiction. Tax laws vary greatly from state to state and change over time. To ensure ongoing compliance and avoid potential penalties or legal issues, S corporations must remain vigilant when monitoring these changes.

Maintaining thorough and accurate records is critical for multi-jurisdictional compliance. S corporations should keep detailed records of their income, expenses, sales transactions, and other financial data that is specific to their jurisdiction. These records serve as the foundation for tax calculations, audits, and any potential tax authority inquiries.

It is strongly advised to retain the services of qualified tax professionals who specialize in multi-jurisdictional tax compliance. These professionals can advise on compliance requirements, assist with tax filings, and guide you through the complexities of reporting obligations across jurisdictions.

S corporations can operate smoothly and avoid penalties or legal consequences by diligently adhering to compliance requirements and reporting obligations. Understanding each jurisdiction's specific compliance obligations, staying up-to-date on tax law changes, and keeping accurate records are all critical components of successful multi-jurisdictional tax compliance for S corporations.

14.6 Evaluating the impact of state and local tax credits and incentives on S corporation tax planning

State and local governments frequently offer tax breaks and credits in order to draw businesses and promote economic growth. This section examines the impact of these tax breaks and credits on S corporation tax planning. S corporation owners can optimize their tax planning strategies and improve their overall tax position by carefully assessing and utilizing these opportunities.

Tax breaks, exemptions, deductions, and credits tailored to specific industries or activities are all examples of tax breaks and credits. These incentives are intended to encourage investment, job creation, R&D, environmental sustainability, and other beneficial activities.

S-corporation owners should thoroughly evaluate the tax incentives and credits available in the jurisdictions where they operate when developing tax planning strategies. This entails investigating and comprehending the eligibility criteria, application procedures, and potential benefits of each incentive or credit program.

S corporations can reduce their tax liabilities, increase cash flow, and allocate resources more effectively by leveraging these incentives and credits. An S corporation, for example, may be eligible for a tax credit based on the creation of new jobs in a specific jurisdiction. By utilizing this credit, the corporation can reduce its tax liability and potentially reinvest the funds saved back into the business.

To ensure compliance and maximize benefits, it is critical to carefully review the terms and conditions of each incentive or credit program. Some incentives may have specific requirements regarding operation duration, employment thresholds, capital investment amounts, or other qualifying factors. Understanding these prerequisites is critical for determining the viability and potential value of each incentive or credit opportunity.

Owners of S corporations should also consider the interaction between federal and state or local tax breaks. In some cases, a state tax incentive or credit may affect the availability or calculation of certain federal tax benefits. To ensure comprehensive tax planning and optimization, it is critical to assess how these incentives interact.

Tax professionals who specialize in state and local tax planning can provide invaluable expertise and guidance. These professionals can assist in evaluating the impact of tax breaks and credits on S corporation tax planning, identifying the most advantageous opportunities, and ensuring program compliance.

S corporation owners can optimize their tax planning strategies, reduce tax burdens, and strengthen their financial position by proactively evaluating and leveraging state and local tax incentives and credits. Taking advantage of these opportunities can provide a competitive advantage and contribute to the S corporation's long-term success.

14.7 Addressing the difficulties and common pitfalls of state and local tax compliance

S-corporation owners may find it difficult to comply with state and local tax requirements. This section addresses the most common challenges and pitfalls in state and local tax compliance. S corporation owners can navigate the compliance landscape more successfully if they understand these challenges and implement effective strategies.

One of the most difficult issues is determining nexus, which refers to the degree of connection or presence a corporation has in a specific state that triggers tax obligations. Nexus laws vary from one jurisdiction to the next and may depend on things like physical presence, economic activity, or sales thresholds. Owners of S corporations must carefully evaluate their business activities in each state to determine if nexus exists and to comply with the corresponding tax obligations.

Another challenge is navigating the varying tax laws of different states. Each state has its own set of tax laws, regulations, and provisions that can differ greatly from federal tax laws. Owners of S corporations must become familiar with the specific tax rules that apply in the states where they operate and ensure compliance with state-level requirements.

Another area of complexity is multistate apportionment. Many states require S corporations to divide their profits among multiple jurisdictions based on factors such as sales, payroll, or property. Accurately calculating and allocating income can be difficult, especially when different states use different apportionment methods. Owners of S corporations must understand the apportionment rules in each state and ensure proper income reporting and allocation.

S-corporation owners can use a variety of strategies to address these issues and avoid common pitfalls. To begin, it is critical to stay current on state and local tax laws and regulations. Monitoring changes on a regular basis and seeking professional advice can help ensure compliance and prevent potential compliance gaps.

It is strongly advised to retain the services of tax professionals who are knowledgeable about state and local tax compliance. These professionals can help with nexus determination, interpretation of state tax laws, multistate apportionment calculations, and navigating the complexities of compliance.

Keeping accurate and well-organized records is critical for state and local tax compliance. Proper documentation of business activities, sales transactions, payroll records, and other pertinent data will facilitate accurate reporting and reduce the risk of errors or discrepancies.

Finally, S corporation owners should think about using technology and specialized tax software to automate compliance processes. Tax software can automate calculations, track changes in tax laws, and help with reporting requirements, saving time and lowering the possibility of errors.

S corporation owners can navigate state and local tax compliance more efficiently if they address these challenges and implement effective strategies. This proactive approach ensures compliance with jurisdiction-specific requirements, reduces compliance risks, and aids in the maintenance of a strong and compliant tax position.

14.8 Case studies demonstrating the application of state and local tax considerations in the taxation of S corporations

In this section, we present case studies that demonstrate the practical application of state and local tax considerations in S corporation taxation. These real-world examples provide valuable insights into how different scenarios can affect tax outcomes and emphasize the importance of state and local tax planning for S corporation owners.

Case Study 1: Tax Obligations and Nexus Determination

In this case study, we look at a scenario in which a S corporation operates in multiple states and must determine nexus and meet tax obligations. We investigate the criteria used by each state to establish nexus and discuss how nexus affects the corporation's tax liabilities. S corporation owners can gain a better understanding of the factors that contribute to nexus determination and the corresponding compliance requirements by reading this case study.

Case Study 2: Income Allocation and Multistate Apportionment

In this case study, we look at the complexities of multistate apportionment for an S corporation that does business in multiple states. We examine the various apportionment methods used by various states and show how these methods affect the allocation of income across states. S corporation owners can understand the complexities of multistate apportionment and learn strategies for accurate income allocation by studying the case study.

Case Study 3: State-Specific Tax Credits and Incentives

This case study focuses on an S corporation's use of state-specific tax breaks and credits. We consider a scenario in which a corporation takes advantage of tax breaks provided by a specific state to reduce its tax liabilities. We go over the eligibility criteria, application process, and potential tax savings from using these incentives strategically. Through this case study, S corporation owners can learn about the benefits of state-specific tax incentives and credits, as well as how to effectively leverage them.

Case Study 4: Compliance Issues and Solutions

In this case study, we look at the compliance issues that an S corporation faces when operating in multiple jurisdictions. We look at common pitfalls like staying up-to-date on changing tax laws, meeting reporting requirements, and navigating state-specific compliance requirements. We present practical solutions and best practices for dealing with these issues and ensuring compliance across multiple states. S corporation owners can learn from real-life examples and apply effective compliance strategies to their own situations by studying this case study.

These case studies serve as practical examples of the complexities and considerations involved in S-corporation state and local tax planning. S corporation owners can gain valuable insights into the application of state and local tax considerations, make informed decisions, and effectively optimize their tax positions by analyzing these scenarios and understanding the outcomes.

Conclusion

Finally, the case studies presented in this chapter are useful tools for understanding how state and local tax considerations are applied in S corporation taxation. These real-world examples offer owners a deeper understanding of the practical implications of state and local tax planning by providing practical insights into how various scenarios can influence tax outcomes.

S corporation owners can gain knowledge and insights that will help them navigate the complexities of state and local taxes more effectively by studying these case studies. They can learn from others' mistakes and apply what they've learned to their own tax planning strategies. Thesc case studies emphasize the significance of considering state and local tax factors and offer owners practical advice on minimizing tax burdens, ensuring compliance, and optimizing their overall tax positions.

S corporation owners can make informed decisions, take advantage of available opportunities, and effectively manage their state and local tax obligations by incorporating the lessons from these case studies into their own tax planning efforts. Owners can confidently navigate the complexities of the tax landscape and achieve greater financial success for their S corporations if they have a thorough understanding of state and local tax considerations.

Chapter 15: International Tax Planning for S Corporation Owners

Introduction

In an increasingly globalized business environment, S-corporation owners may face unique international tax planning challenges and opportunities. This chapter delves into the complexities of international taxation for S corporations, offering advice on key considerations, compliance requirements, and strategies for achieving the best tax outcomes in the international arena.

Key topics covered in this chapter include:

1. Understanding how international operations affect S corporation tax planning.
2. Identifying a S corporation's presence in foreign jurisdictions and the associated tax obligations.
3. Evaluating tax treaties and their role in preventing double taxation for owners of S corporations.
4. Considerations and strategies for ensuring compliance with international tax rules.
5. Considering the tax implications of foreign investments, including the rules governing controlled foreign corporations (CFCs).
6. Strategies for reinvesting profits from international operations and managing currency exchange risks.
7. S corporations with international activities must comply with certain requirements, including reporting obligations.
8. Real-world examples of international tax considerations and strategies for S corporation owners.

S corporation owners can optimize their global operations, reduce tax liabilities, and effectively manage their international tax obligations by navigating the complexities of international taxation.

15.1 Understanding the Tax Effects of International Operations on S Corporations

This section delves into the implications of international operations for S corporation tax planning. It delves into the potential implications for income sourcing, foreign tax credits, and the S corporation's overall tax position.

When an S corporation conducts international business, it adds a new level of complexity to its tax planning strategies. As the corporation must decide how to allocate income between domestic and foreign sources, the source of income becomes a critical consideration. This determination has the potential to have a significant impact on the corporation's taxable income and the amount of tax owed in each jurisdiction.

Furthermore, foreign tax credits are critical to avoiding double taxation for S corporations that operate on a global scale. Understanding the rules and limitations governing foreign tax credits is critical to optimizing the S corporation's tax position and avoiding the burden of paying taxes on the same income twice.

Several factors influence a S corporation's overall tax position, including the interaction of domestic and foreign tax laws, tax treaties, and the structure of international operations. Owners of S corporations must carefully assess the impact of international operations on their tax liabilities and consider strategies to reduce tax obligations while adhering to both domestic and foreign tax laws.

Owners can make informed decisions about the structure and management of their international activities if they understand the impact of international operations on S corporation tax planning. This knowledge allows them to optimizc their tax positions, effectively navigate cross-border transactions, and maximize the benefits of engaging in global business operations.

15.2 Determining the presence of an S corporation in foreign jurisdictions and the associated tax obligations

This section delves into the criteria used to determine whether an S corporation has a presence in other countries, such as the presence of permanent establishments. It also looks at the potential tax obligations and compliance requirements.

When an S corporation operates in foreign jurisdictions, it is critical to determine whether it has established a presence in those jurisdictions that trigger tax obligations. A permanent establishment is a concept that is commonly used to determine whether an S corporation has a taxable presence in a foreign country. Permanent establishments can be physical locations, such as offices or factories, or specific activities that meet the criteria set forth in local tax laws.

The S corporation is subject to tax obligations in the foreign jurisdiction once the presence of a permanent establishment is established. These responsibilities may include filing tax returns, paying corporate income tax, and adhering to local tax laws and regulations. S-corporation owners must understand and comply with the tax obligations of each foreign jurisdiction in which they have a presence.

Compliance with foreign tax obligations frequently entails navigating complex rules, such as transfer pricing regulations, withholding tax obligations, and documentation requirements. To ensure compliance and reduce the risk of penalties or other negative consequences, S corporation owners must stay informed about each jurisdiction's tax laws and regulations.

Determining an S corporation's presence in foreign jurisdictions and understanding the associated tax obligations is an important step in international tax planning. S corporation owners can effectively operate in foreign markets while complying with local tax laws by accurately assessing their foreign presence and fulfilling their tax obligations.

15.3 Tax treaties and their role in avoiding double taxation for S corporation owners

Tax treaties have a significant impact on reducing double taxation for S corporation owners who conduct cross-border business. This section discusses the significance of tax treaties, their provisions, and how they benefit S corporations by lowering tax liabilities.

Tax treaties are bilateral agreements between two countries to avoid or reduce double taxation on income. These treaties establish rules and guidelines for income taxation and ensure that taxpayers are not taxed twice on the same income in different jurisdictions. Tax treaties provide a framework for determining tax liabilities and allocating taxing rights between the home country and foreign jurisdictions for S corporations with international operations.

Tax treaties typically address a wide range of international tax issues, such as the taxation of business profits, dividends, interest, royalties, and capital gains. They frequently include provisions such as eliminating double taxation, allocating taxing rights, preventing tax evasion and avoidance, and resolving disputes between tax authorities.

S corporation owners can benefit from lower tax burdens by evaluating tax treaties and understanding their provisions. Tax treaties may offer relief through mechanisms such as tax credits, exemptions, lower withholding rates, or the exclusion of certain types of income from taxation in one or both treaty countries. These provisions assist S corporations in avoiding or minimizing the negative effects of double taxation while also promoting fair and efficient cross-border taxation.

S corporation owners must be aware of the tax treaties entered into by their home country and how these treaties interact with the tax laws of the foreign jurisdictions in which they operate. S corporation owners can optimize their international tax position, reduce double taxation, and increase their competitiveness in the global marketplace by leveraging the benefits offered by tax treaties and ensuring compliance with their requirements.

15.4 Transfer pricing considerations and strategies to ensure international tax compliance

Transfer pricing is an important aspect of international taxation that focuses on the pricing of transactions between related entities operating in different tax jurisdictions. This section emphasizes the significance of transfer pricing compliance and investigates strategies that S corporations can use to ensure compliance with international tax rules.

When S corporations conduct transactions with related entities such as subsidiaries or affiliates, transfer prices that reflect the arm's length principle must be established. According to the arm's length principle, the prices or terms of transactions between related entities must be equivalent to those agreed upon between unrelated entities in similar circumstances. This principle ensures that profits are appropriately allocated and that taxation is equitable across jurisdictions.

S corporations should implement effective transfer pricing strategies to ensure compliance with international tax rules. These strategies entail conducting comprehensive transfer pricing analyses, which may include benchmarking studies, economic analyses, and documentation of the pricing methodologies used. S corporations can demonstrate compliance with the arm's length principle by demonstrating that their transfer prices are consistent with market conditions.

Advanced pricing agreements (APAs) with tax authorities should also be considered by S corporations. By allowing taxpayers and tax authorities to agree on transfer pricing methods and pricing adjustments in advance, APAs provide certainty. This proactive approach reduces the risk of transfer pricing disputes while also providing a more stable and predictable tax environment for S corporations operating on a global scale.

Maintaining contemporaneous documentation is another critical aspect of transfer pricing compliance. To demonstrate compliance with applicable tax rules, S corporations should document their transfer pricing policies, methodologies, and supporting analyses. This documentation serves as evidence of their transactions' arm's length nature and provides a strong defense in the event of a tax audit or dispute.

S corporations can navigate the complexities of international taxation, mitigate transfer pricing risks, and ensure that their global transactions are conducted in accordance with international tax rules by prioritizing transfer pricing compliance and employing effective strategies. This not only encourages compliance, but it also improves their reputation, lowers the risk of penalties, and fosters a positive relationship with tax authorities.

15.5 Evaluating the tax implications of foreign investments, including the rules governing controlled foreign corporations (CFCs)

When S corporations make foreign investments, it is critical to consider the tax consequences, especially the application of controlled foreign corporation (CFC) rules. This section explains how CFC rules affect S corporation owners and discusses strategies for managing tax obligations related to foreign investments.

If an S corporation owns or controls a foreign corporation that meets certain criteria, the S corporation may be required to include a portion of the foreign corporation's income in its own taxable income, even if the income has not been distributed, under CFC rules. This is intended to prevent taxpayers from using foreign corporations to defer or avoid paying taxes in the United States.

S corporations must determine whether their foreign investments are subject to CFC rules. The percentage of ownership, the types of income the foreign corporation earns, and particular control tests that the tax authorities have established are all factors that affect how the CFC rules apply. To determine the potential tax impact on the S corporation, it is critical to carefully examine these rules and their thresholds.

S corporations can use a variety of strategies to manage their tax obligations related to foreign investments and CFC rules. Consider structuring investments in such a way that CFC classification is minimized. This might entail altering ownership stakes, reorganizing corporate structures, or reviewing the sources of income the foreign corporation generates.

S corporations can also consider using foreign tax credits to offset any U.S. tax liabilities caused by CFC rules. Taxpayers can claim a credit for taxes paid to foreign jurisdictions, reducing their overall tax liability in the United States. S corporations can effectively manage their tax obligations related to foreign investments by carefully assessing the availability and limitations of foreign tax credits.

S corporations should also stay current on changes in CFC rules and tax regulations to ensure ongoing compliance. The tax landscape for foreign investments is constantly changing, and new legislation or regulatory developments may have an impact on how CFC rules are applied. S corporations can adapt their strategies and stay compliant with the latest requirements by staying informed and working with tax professionals.

S corporation owners can proactively manage their tax obligations and optimize their international tax planning by assessing the tax implications of foreign investments, including the application of CFC rules. S corporations can navigate the complexities of foreign investments and ensure tax compliance by using strategic structuring, utilizing foreign tax credits, and staying informed about regulatory changes.

15.6 Strategies for repatriating profits and managing currency exchange risks

Profits from foreign operations must be repatriated, and currency exchange risks must be effectively managed for S corporation owners doing international business. This section delves into strategies for facilitating profit repatriation while mitigating currency exchange risks in order to maximize tax outcomes.

When it comes to repatriating profits, S corporation owners should carefully consider the most tax-effective options. To repatriate profits, one strategy is to use dividends or distributions from foreign subsidiaries. The tax consequences of these methods, however, may differ depending on factors such as tax treaties, local tax laws, and the structure of the foreign subsidiaries.

Another option for repatriating profits is to consider intercompany loans or royalty payments. S corporations can strike a balance between repatriating profits and effectively managing tax liabilities by structuring these transactions appropriately and ensuring they comply with transfer pricing rules.

When dealing with foreign operations, currency exchange risks must be considered. Exchange rate fluctuations can affect the value of repatriated profits, affecting the overall tax outcome for S corporations. S corporation owners can use a variety of strategies to manage these risks.

Hedging instruments such as currency futures or options are a common approach. These financial instruments enable S corporations to protect themselves from adverse currency movements, potentially reducing the impact on repatriated profits. To assess the suitability and effectiveness of hedging strategies, it is critical to collaborate closely with financial professionals and advisors.

Another option is to think about centralized treasury management. S corporations can optimize currency exchange activities, reduce transaction costs, and manage foreign currency holdings more efficiently by centralizing cash management and employing techniques such as netting or cash pooling.

S corporation owners must stay up to date on all currency exchange rates, economic trends, and geopolitical developments that might have an impact on currency markets. They can make informed decisions and adjust their strategies by monitoring and analyzing these factors.

Furthermore, S corporations should consider the potential tax consequences of currency exchange gains or losses. Tax rules vary by jurisdiction, so it is critical to understand the tax treatment of currency gains and losses when repatriating profits.

S corporation owners can optimize their tax outcomes and ensure the efficient use of their international earnings by implementing strategies for repatriating profits from foreign operations and effectively managing currency exchange risks. S corporations can navigate the complexities of international business and minimize the impact of currency exchange risks on their overall tax position by assessing the most appropriate repatriation methods, employing hedging strategies, considering centralized treasury management, and staying informed about currency markets.

15.7 Compliance obligations for S corporations with international operations, including reporting requirements

Operating on a global scale necessitates specific compliance and reporting obligations for S corporations. This section provides an overview of the key compliance obligations that must be met in order to comply with international tax laws and regulations.

The proper documentation and maintenance of transfer pricing records are critical compliance requirements for S corporations with international operations. The pricing of transactions between related entities in different jurisdictions is referred to as transfer pricing. S corporations must create and keep documentation proving the arm's length nature of their intercompany transactions. This documentation should include specifics about the pricing methodology, comparable transactions, and the analysis that supports the transfer pricing decisions.

The filing of international information reports is another important compliance requirement. Form 5471 (Information Return of U.S. Persons With Respect to Certain Foreign Corporations), Form 8858 (Information Return of U.S. Persons With Respect to Foreign Disregarded Entities), or Form 8865 (Return of U.S. Persons With Respect to Certain Foreign Partnerships) may be required of S corporations engaged in cross-border transactions. These forms collect and provide information to tax authorities about the S corporation's foreign investments, subsidiaries, partnerships, or disregarded entities.

Furthermore, S corporations with foreign operations must ensure compliance with local tax laws. Each jurisdiction may have its own tax filing and reporting requirements, such as the submission of annual tax returns, financial statements, or other information requested by local tax authorities. To remain in compliance in each jurisdiction in which they operate, S corporations must understand and fulfill these obligations.

S corporations may retain the services of international tax professionals who specialize in navigating the complexities of international tax laws to assist with compliance. These professionals can advise on compliance obligations, assist with transfer pricing documentation, and ensure that international information reports are filed on time and accurately.

S corporations must keep current with changes in international tax laws and regulations. International tax laws are updated and modified on a regular basis, and S corporations must be aware of any new reporting requirements or compliance obligations that may arise.

S corporations can operate within the framework of international tax laws, maintain transparency, and demonstrate their commitment to compliance by meeting the compliance requirements and reporting obligations associated with international activities. Following these obligations not only helps S corporations avoid penalties and potential audits, but it also builds trust with tax authorities and contributes to the overall success and sustainability of their international operations.

15.8 Real-world examples of international tax considerations and strategies for S corporation owners

We present real-life examples of international tax planning considerations and strategies for S corporation owners to improve understanding and practical application. These examples demonstrate how various scenarios can affect tax outcomes and provide useful insights into effective international tax planning.

Example 1: Entering a New Market

An S corporation decides to establish a subsidiary in order to expand its operations into a foreign market. The example demonstrates the considerations involved in subsidiary structuring, such as selecting an appropriate legal entity, evaluating the tax implications of different jurisdictions, and utilizing tax treaties to avoid double taxation. It also emphasizes the significance of transfer pricing compliance and the methods used to ensure arm's length pricing in intercompany transactions.

Example 2: Repatriating Foreign Profits

In this case, an S corporation has accumulated profits in its foreign subsidiary and wishes to repatriate them to the United States. The example investigates the various repatriation strategies available, such as dividend distributions, loans, or intercompany services, and analyzes the tax implications of each approach. It also covers the impact of currency exchange rates as well as the strategies used to manage currency risks during the repatriation process.

Example 3: Managing Controlled Foreign Corporation (CFC) Regulations

An S corporation owns stock in a foreign corporation that meets the definition of a Controlled Foreign Corporation (CFC). This example examines the tax implications of CFC rules, such as the inclusion of Subpart F income, the use of the GILTI (Global Intangible Low-Taxed Income) regime, and the potential availability of foreign tax credits. It demonstrates how S corporation owners can navigate these rules in order to optimize their tax position and lessen the impact of CFC regulations.

Example 4: Compliance with International Reporting Requirements

In this case, an S corporation has multiple foreign subsidiaries that must comply with various reporting requirements. The example shows the complexities of international reporting obligations, such as filing Form 5471 for foreign subsidiaries, adhering to country-specific financial statement requirements, and maintaining proper documentation for transfer pricing compliance. It emphasizes the significance of timely and accurate reporting in order to comply with international tax laws.

These case studies offer practical insights into the international tax planning considerations and strategies that S corporation owners may face. S corporation owners can make informed decisions, optimize their international tax planning strategies, and effectively navigate the complexities of international taxation by studying these scenarios and understanding the associated tax implications.

Conclusion

To optimize their global operations, minimize tax liabilities, and effectively manage their international tax obligations, S corporation owners must navigate the complexities of international taxation. This chapter has provided a thorough understanding of international tax planning considerations and strategies that can assist S corporation owners in their international ventures.

S corporation owners can proactively optimize their tax outcomes in the international arena by understanding the impact of international operations on tax planning, determining their presence in foreign jurisdictions, leveraging tax treaties to mitigate double taxation, ensuring transfer pricing compliance, assessing the tax implications of foreign investments, and employing strategies for profit repatriation and currency exchange risk management.

Furthermore, understanding and fulfilling compliance requirements and reporting obligations for S corporations with international operations is critical to maintaining compliance with international tax laws and regulations. S corporation owners can avoid penalties and maintain cross-border compliance by staying up-to-date on international reporting obligations and diligently fulfilling them.

Throughout this chapter, real-life examples have demonstrated the practical application of international tax planning considerations and strategies. S corporation owners can make informed decisions and effectively manage their international tax planning by studying these examples and gaining insights into the impact of different scenarios on tax outcomes.

S corporation owners can confidently expand their business presence globally if they have a thorough understanding of international tax planning considerations and the strategies discussed in this chapter. S corporation owners can successfully navigate the complexities of international taxation and thrive in the global marketplace by maintaining compliance, optimizing tax benefits, and strategically managing their international tax obligations.

Epilogue: S Corporation Tax Secrets Checklist

Well done on finishing "S Corporation Tax Secrets"!

As you embark on your journey through S corporation taxation, here's a handy checklist summarizing the key takeaways and actionable steps to optimize your tax planning and compliance efforts:

1. Determine S Corporation Eligibility:
   - Confirm that your business meets the eligibility requirements for S corporation status.
   - Submit Form 2553 with the IRS to elect S corporation status.

2. Understand Tax Advantages:
   - Familiarize yourself with the tax advantages of S corporations, including pass-through taxation and potential tax savings.

3. Maintain Reasonable Compensation:
   - Set reasonable compensation for shareholder-employees to ensure compliance and avoid IRS scrutiny.
   - Consider factors such as industry standards, job responsibilities, and financial performance.

4. Leverage the Qualified Business Income Deduction:

- Take advantage of the qualified business income deduction available to eligible S corporation owners.

- Ensure your business qualifies and optimize your deduction by maximizing wages and/or qualified property.

5. Implement Tax Planning Strategies:
   - Explore various tax planning strategies, such as timing income and expenses, maximizing deductible expenses, and utilizing tax credits.

   - Consider the impact of state and local taxes, economic factors, and changes in tax laws on your tax planning.

6. Regularly Review and Update:
   - Conduct regular reviews of your tax planning strategies to adapt to changing circumstances and optimize your tax position.

   - Stay informed about tax law updates and consult with tax professionals to interpret and apply new rules.

7. International Tax Considerations:
   - Understand the impact of international operations on S corporation tax planning.

   - Evaluate the presence in foreign jurisdictions, assess tax treaties, comply with transfer pricing rules, and manage tax implications of foreign investments.

8. Stay Compliant:
   - Fulfill compliance requirements and reporting obligations for S corporations, including state and local

taxes, international activities, and reporting to regulatory authorities.

- Maintain organized records and documentation to support your tax positions.

9. Seek Professional Advice:
   - Engage with qualified tax professionals who specialize in S corporation taxation.

   - Consult experts to ensure accuracy, compliance, and optimize your tax planning strategies.

10. Monitor and Adapt:
    - Stay updated on tax law changes, regulatory updates, and emerging tax planning opportunities.

    - Continuously monitor your financial situation, business growth, and evolving tax landscape to adapt your strategies accordingly.

By following this checklist and implementing the strategies and insights shared in "S Corporation Tax Secrets," you are well-equipped to navigate the complexities of S corporation taxation, minimize tax liabilities, and maximize your tax benefits. Remember, ongoing education, compliance, and strategic planning are the keys to achieving long-term success in managing your S corporation's tax affairs. Best of luck on your journey to tax optimization and financial success!

Made in the USA
Las Vegas, NV
22 September 2023

77928662R10157